The Selma Campaign

The Selma Campaign

Martin Luther King Jr., Jimmie Lee Jackson, and the Defining Struggle of the Civil Rights Era

CRAIG SWANSON

Archway Publishing books may be ordered through booksellers or by contacting:

Archway Publishing
1663 Liberty Drive
Bloomington, IN 47403
www.archwaypublishing.com
1-(888)-242-5904

Cover photo courtesy of
the Associated Press, New York, N.Y.

ISBN: 978-1-4808-1210-9 (sc)
ISBN: 978-1-4808-1212-3 (hc)
ISBN: 978-1-4808-1211-6 (e)

Library of Congress Control Number: 2014919124

Printed in the United States of America.

Archway Publishing rev. date: 11/14/14

For Amy, Jon, and Eric

Acknowledgment

This book never would have made it to print without the superb editing job of my youngest son, Eric Swanson. Eric's profound understanding of grammar, style, and syntax made *The Selma Campaign* much better and easier to read. I am deeply grateful to him and look forward to returning the favor.

Contents

Preface

Of all the repressive Jim Crow laws that ruled the South for much of the post-Civil War era, few were as nefarious as those that served to suppress the black vote. African-Americans attempting to register were forced to contend with an array of extra-legal tactics developed by southern officials to ensure white political and economic supremacy.

The Fifteenth Amendment to the U.S. Constitution, adopted in 1870, guaranteed the right to vote to all male citizens, stating simply:

"The right of citizens of the United States to vote shall not be denied or abridged by the United States or by any State on account of race, color, or previous condition of servitude." Following years of struggle, women would receive that same right in 1920.

As a broad statement of principle, the Fifteenth Amendment was direct and unambiguous, but its intent was easily circumvented by segregationist southern lawmakers, who implemented cynical measures, such as literacy tests and poll taxes, to thwart would-be black voters without actually referencing their race.

The Civil Rights Act of 1964, which sought to bar unequal application of voting laws, was a bit more problematic from the white power structure's point of view, but it too was easily neutered by crafty politicians, who parsed the wording for legal loopholes and malleable sentiments that could be contorted and reshaped to fit their desires. Many of these interpretations skated to the edge of legal compliance, and sometimes beyond, but that was of little concern to those entrusted with protecting the "southern way of life." For years, they had managed to violate the spirit if not the actual letter of civil rights laws with little negative backlash, and they weren't about to concede now, especially on an issue as potentially disruptive as the black vote.

Many white folks felt it was bad enough that they now had to share a lunch counter or drinking fountain with their black brethren, per the Civil Rights Act, but allowing blacks to vote? That was unthinkable. Doing so would be more than a simple "accommodation," they feared; it likely would hasten the demise of the South's entire economic and social structure.

Their concerns were not without merit. Black residents comprised some 25 to 30 percent of the Deep South's population in the mid-60s. A committed black electorate on an even playing field could seriously disrupt if not destroy the cherished traditions and institutions that southerners – white southerners – held dear. Over time, more and more black residents would be elected to public office, and once there they presumably would pursue the cause of racial equality, not just under the law but in actual practice.

The potential consequences were enormous. For wealthy white businessmen, planters and industrialists, it would mean an end to years of cheap labor. For members of the white working class, it would mean competition for better jobs, and also would threaten their artificially inflated social standing. With no permanent black underclass, uneducated whites risked losing what little socioeconomic status they had.

As the Mississippi Summer Project of 1964 revealed, the South was prepared to resist these changes forcefully and, if need be, violently. White Mississippi employed tactics ranging from verbal threats to physical intimidation and deadly violence in a brutal, unofficially sanctioned campaign to deter the racial rabble-rousers.

So-called "Freedom Summer" volunteers and local black residents were subjected to drive-by shootings, Molotov cocktail bombings, and constant threats. State and local governments, police, and white supremacist organizations, including the Ku Klux Klan, used murder, arrests, beatings, arson, and other forms of harassment to sabotage the campaign.

The intimidation strategy was legally and morally indefensible, but the terror it engendered was palpable and impossible to overcome. No more than a handful of black voters were registered.

Conventional wisdom held that the Mississippi movement had failed. Black leaders were in retreat, and white supremacists were confident they would again prevail when the campaign moved elsewhere, if indeed there was to be another effort. But that was a mistake born of hubris and misplaced southern pride.

The campaign might not have succeeded in filling Mississippi voting rolls with black registrants, its main objective, but it did heighten public awareness of racial discrimination. Extensive media coverage of the events occurring in Mississippi led to greater scrutiny of future campaigns, transforming what had been a primarily regional dispute into one with national implications. Much of Middle America was repulsed by the brutality it witnessed, and people who until then had paid little attention to reports of racial strife began to stir uneasily.

Shifting public sentiment would be critical to the drive for black voting rights, and movement leaders now had to determine how best to harness the support they were beginning to receive.

Their next big test would come in Selma, Alabama, Queen City of the Black Belt. It would prove to be the defining campaign of the civil rights era.

Selma is sacred ground to civil rights advocates, and those who conducted the 1965 campaign there – Martin Luther King, Ralph Abernathy, Andrew Young, John Lewis, James Bevel, and other movement stalwarts – are rightfully credited with guiding the mission to success, despite bitter, sometimes violent opposition and fractious internal disputes.

But the campaign never would have had such a remarkable impact without committed support from the residents of nearby Marion, a small town seething with Jim Crow-era racial animus. It was in Marion that a trigger-happy Alabama State Patrol trooper shot an unarmed black man in February 1965, a pivotal incident that set in motion a chain of events that would usher America into a brave new world of race relations.

This book chronicles the Selma/Marion Voting Rights campaign, beginning with King's decision to bring his forces to the Black Belt in early 1965 and concluding nearly five decades later with the resolution of criminal proceedings against the Alabama state trooper who fired the shot that killed Jimmie Lee Jackson.

Chapter 1: The Year of the Vote

Rev. Martin Luther King Jr. was resting in an Atlanta hospital bed when he got the news. It was October 14, 1964. A day earlier, King had collapsed of a viral infection and exhaustion after delivering six speeches in four cities over the previous seventy-two hours.

King's doctor insisted that he get some much-needed bed rest, and the headstrong civil rights leader finally acquiesced, admitting himself to St. Joseph's Infirmary late in the afternoon of October 13. There, with the assistance of a potent sleeping pill, King quickly drifted into a sound sleep.

A jangling bedside telephone woke him early the next morning. Groggy from his long night's rest, King fumbled for the receiver. He sleepily acknowledged his wife, Coretta, but her message jolted him awake.

King had been chosen to receive the 1964 Nobel Peace Prize for his tireless work on behalf of civil rights and social justice. Although the announcement was not entirely unexpected, the news took King by surprise. Climbing out of bed, he quickly dressed and mentally prepped himself for the long day ahead. Coretta's message had arrived just in time. In a matter of minutes, the hospital was overrun by reporters, photographers, and TV cameramen. [1]

Though the Nobel Prize was special, it was not King's first prestigious honor. Less than a year earlier, he had been named *Time Magazine*'s 1963 Man of the Year. It was heady stuff for the 35-year-old son of a southern Baptist preacher, but as with most things, King took the Nobel announcement in stride, crediting the Civil Rights movement at large for the accolade and downplaying his own role. The Nobel Prize, he said, was evidence of international support for the entire movement, not just his personal role in it.

King eagerly anticipated the award presentation ceremony scheduled for December 10 in Oslo, Norway, not only to collect his prize – in fact, he had already announced that he would donate his prize money of more than $54,000 to various movement organizations – but also because it would give him a prominent platform for his singular message on civil rights.

In Oslo, King promoted his vision of nonviolent protest as "the answer to the crucial political and moral issue of our time," and called his award "profound recognition of the need for man to overcome oppression and violence without resorting to violence and oppression."

King also reinforced his commitment to the practice and referenced its progenitor, Mahatma Gandhi, saying, "Civilization and violence are antithetical concepts. Negroes of the United States, following the people of India, have demonstrated that nonviolence is not sterile passivity, but a powerful moral force, which makes for social transformation."

Concluding his speech on an optimistic note, he said, "I accept this award today with an abiding faith in America and an audacious faith in the future of mankind."[2]

But even as he spoke, King knew that his professed faith in the nonviolence doctrine would be tested many times in the coming months and thus viewed the prize not as a symbol of success but as a reminder of the work yet to be done.

Unlike the *Time Magazine* honor, which King had cavalierly dismissed as insignificant, the Nobel Prize seemed to heighten his sense of purpose. "History has thrust me into this position," he told reporters the day after the award was announced. "It would both be immoral and a sign of ingratitude if I did not face my moral responsibility to do what I can in this struggle."[3]

His work was waiting, and King was eager to get started.

With the Nobel ceremonies behind him and 1964 drawing to a close, King immersed himself in planning the movement's next major project. Like Freedom Summer, the Birmingham, Alabama, anti-segregation campaign of 1963 and the St. Augustine, Florida, campaign of mid-1964 had not only heightened awareness of the many indignities suffered by black Americans but also resulted in tangible progress, leading directly to the U.S. Civil Rights Act of 1964.

Though successful in having achieved their limited goals, the Birmingham and St. Augustine campaigns – both of which were conceived and conducted by King and the organization he headed, the Southern Christian Leadership Conference (SCLC) --failed to change the social or political dynamic of the South. Significant as they were, these campaigns improved local conditions and heightened public awareness of the plight of southern blacks, but true equality for all was still a distant dream.

Despite the inevitable ups and downs, King and his advisors were pleased with the outcome of both campaigns and consequent approval of the Civil Rights Act, but they also knew they had a long way to go. Indeed, just a few short months after its adoption, the Civil Rights Act was already being circumvented by southern segregationists, some of whom wriggled through loopholes in the law and others who blatantly defied it, loopholes or not.

Signed into law by President Lyndon Johnson on July 2, 1964, the act was designed to be a broad and thorough attack on segregation, outlawing racial discrimination in education, public accommodations, and employment. It was a solid first step, but it didn't go far enough, especially in the area of voting rights, and its lack of any substantial enforcement mechanisms emboldened defiant southerners to delay implementation and/or employ a wide range of under-handed schemes to ensure that black residents would remain confined to second-class status.[4]

Still, it was progress, and King's job now was to build on the foundation the act established. The laws of the land, he determined, would be only as good as the people charged with enforcing them, but since the vast majority of black southerners were now systematically prevented from voting, they would have no say in who would interpret those laws or how they would be applied.

That would have to change.

Not surprisingly, the most prominent civil rights campaign of 1964 was also the bloodiest.

Freedom Summer in Mississippi was beset with violent opposition from the beginning. Indeed, the campaign had barely begun before three civil rights workers disappeared while traveling through Neshoba County. The bodies of James Chaney, Michael Schwerner and Andrew Goodman were discovered in an earthen dam on a farm near Philadelphia, Mississippi, later that summer. The deaths of the three young men highlighted the fact that the campaign produced almost as many acts of violence by whites as it did new black voters. A subsequent study revealed that Freedom Summer produced 6 murders, 35 shooting incidents with 3 injured, 30 homes and other buildings bombed, 35 churches burned, and 80 people beaten.[5]

Although King's Southern Christian Leadership Conference was not directly involved with the Freedom Summer campaign, King took note of the difficulties being experienced by COFO volunteers, saying, "Our nation sent out Peace Corps volunteers throughout the under-developed nations of the world and none of them experienced the kind of brutality and savagery that these voter registration workers have suffered in Mississippi."

By late 1964, civil rights leaders and foot soldiers alike were exhausted after the bruising campaigns in Mississippi, Alabama, and Florida, but most – encouraged by the slow but steady progress being made – were eager to push forward.

King thus wasn't worried about the commitment of his followers, but instead fretted over the direction of the movement itself. While not always successful, previous campaigns had yielded some valuable lessons that King was determined to exploit. A largely peaceful and undramatic initiative in Albany, Georgia, in 1961-62 failed to create significant national interest and did little to advance the movement's cause. Conversely, the confrontational Birmingham campaign of 1963, in which authorities used fire hoses and police attack dogs to restrain vulnerable marchers, generated national headlines and vivid television news reports, resulting in an important public relations victory for the protesters.

Taken with the experiences of Freedom Summer, the conclusion was inescapable: Unprovoked white violence aimed at unresisting black demonstrators was essential to create national interest and support. Equally important, King deduced that a single, easily explainable goal would be preferable to a list of demands that were not conducive to quick and simple presentation.[6]

At an SCLC banquet in October 1964, King called for "profound and revolutionary changes" to address his belief that political inequality went far beyond segregated schools and bus terminals. In Alabama, he told his audience, it would take 135 years to register 10,000 black voters under the existing system.[7]

And on Wednesday, November 4, the day after President Johnson's resounding election victory over Republican challenger Barry Goldwater, King announced plans to renew demonstrations aimed directly at the right to vote.

Just one week later, at an SCLC planning retreat in Birmingham, King aide James Bevel proposed Selma, Alabama, as a test city for a mass movement dedicated to voting rights. Bevel's idea was applauded by Amelia Boynton of Selma's Dallas County Voter's League, which, fortuitously, had sent a delegation to the retreat in hopes of eliciting support from the SCLC.

Disenchanted with the slow pace of voter registration progress in Selma, the Dallas County seat, Boynton and her colleagues formally sought SCLC intervention. The voting rolls in Selma weren't expanding, they said, and the situation for black residents was more desperate than ever.

Most movement leaders agreed that meaningful, lasting social change would occur only when blacks could play a much larger role in the electoral process. Without the vote, they knew, African-Americans would forever be at the mercy of racist politicians and a power structure intent on maintaining white supremacy. But while in accord on the goal, organizers were split as to how it could best be achieved. Many favored some version of the community organizing approach used in Mississippi, but King was convinced that voting rights for southern blacks could be secured and protected only through direct federal government action, not interminable community-by-community campaigns. The high cost and discouraging results of Freedom Summer underscored his belief, as did the energy and effort expended to secure modest changes in Birmingham and St. Augustine.

Much better, King believed, would be a campaign with a broader purpose, one that, if successful, would eliminate the need for a grinding succession of campaigns by ensuring black Americans not just the right to vote but the *ability* to vote. Armed with the means to register voters without the interference of Jim Crow laws and supported by the full legal authority of the federal government, southern blacks would soon be able to effect significant change through the ballot box instead of the street protest. Or so the reasoning went.

Newly elected President Johnson agreed with King's assessment, but the depth of his commitment was uncertain. Johnson signaled his support for a comprehensive voters rights bill during a White House meeting with King in November 1964, but told him it was not yet time to act. He appeared eager to proceed but didn't want to risk offending Southern congressmen, whose votes he would need for his Great Society programs. Still, Johnson assured King of his support, and, as the meeting was breaking up asked him to provide political cover by generating public support. "Now, Dr. King," Johnson drawled, "you go out there and make it possible for me to do the right thing."[8]

Although disappointed by the lack of immediate government action, King was encouraged by the President's response and told friends and colleagues he believed the President was determined to forge ahead. In the year or so since Johnson had assumed the presidency following the assassination of John F. Kennedy, he and King had developed a respectful, if wary, relationship. King believed he could work with the President. And Johnson, while sometimes annoyed by King's stubbornness and perceived lack of patience, shared the civil rights leader's vision, and admired his commitment to the cause.

Their relationship, while not always smooth, would be key to the voting rights campaign.

Unlike previous campaigns, which often contained a surfeit of demands mostly in regard to local conditions – the right of a person to ride the bus, visit the theater, or sit at the lunch counter – King wanted his next project to focus on a single, easily understood goal, one with broad and lasting implications. Simply put, he wanted a law that would make it impossible for southern states to prevent black residents from registering to vote. This was more than asking for an accommodation; it was demanding a fundamental constitutional right.

As Andrew Young, one of King's chief lieutenants, said, "To really change the South, it was necessary for the 'Colored' signs to come down, but it was also necessary to elect men and women of goodwill to public office." Justice, Young said, had to be institutionalized into the body politic and not experienced just as a response to the pressure of demonstrations and boycotts.[9]

The Civil Rights Act of 1964 did, in fact, contain a section devoted to voting rights but it was doomed by the absence of a sturdy enforcement mechanism. The biggest problem for potential black voters was the Act's failure to adequately address the widespread use of screening devices called "literacy tests." Ostensibly designed to determine one's mental fitness to vote, the easily manipulated tests, along with poll taxes and physical intimidation, were critical to suppression of black voting rights. The tests were structured and administered in a variety of creative ways, all but ensuring that illiterate white southerners would pass but even the most highly educated blacks were destined to fail. For instance, a loophole was created allowing whites to pass at the discretion of county test-givers. Also, Alabama law was written so that potential voters whose grandfathers voted during or immediately after the Civil War were eligible to vote without having to pay the poll tax or pass the literacy test.

The Civil Rights Act didn't ban these tests, declaring only that they couldn't be used arbitrarily. And enforcement was weak. The Justice Department was empowered to sue only on behalf of individuals who were discriminated against when attempting to register, meaning a separate lawsuit had to be filed for each of the thousands of people claiming discrimination.

Years later, Annie Ward of Marion, Alabama, said she failed the test but was never told what questions she allegedly got wrong. "They said I didn't pass," she recalled bitterly. "I don't remember the specific questions, but it was a whole lot of unnecessary information about things that weren't important or related to the right to vote."

If Ward, who had a college degree at the time, couldn't pass, the prospects weren't good for less-educated African-Americans.

In addition to these discriminatory impediments, white southerners didn't hesitate to use violence to prohibit the black vote. Hate-driven organizations such as the Ku Klux Klan waged campaigns of terror against blacks, threatening and intimidating potential voters and often resorting to violence. These white vigilantes were responsible for some 4,500 lynchings in the United States from the 1880s through the 1950s.

As the SCLC was mapping out plans to make 1965 the year of the vote, King's thoughts kept returning to Selma. He was very much aware of the city's hyper-racist reputation and the dangers it presented, but was also beginning to warm to Bevel's plan to target Selma for direct action. The more he thought about the idea, the more he liked it. Reckless, overly aggressive opposition had helped the movement in Birmingham, King mused, perhaps the same would hold true for Selma.

In public, King appeared relaxed and confident. The Nobel Prize ceremony and attendant hoopla had not only validated his organization, it had reinvigorated him personally. In private, however, he and others were beginning to worry that political concerns might cause President Johnson to delay, or even postpone, the introduction of voting rights legislation.

Chapter 2: 'One hell of a field general'

King, like most civil rights leaders, trusted President Johnson, but only so far. During his short time as president, Johnson had proven to be a valuable ally. Still, his segregationist past as a Texas congressman troubled those with long memories. Johnson was seen as a recent convert to the civil rights cause, and many questioned the depth of his support. More worrisome, the President had been silent on the issue of civil rights since his November meeting with King. Johnson subsequently had announced that he would focus on "urban problems," but emphasized conservation, education, and industry tax credits. There was no immediate mention of civil rights.[1]

Johnson and King didn't talk again until mid-January. With Johnson busy on a number of post-election fronts and King focused on Selma planning, the lack of contact was not surprising, but the nearly two-month communications gap did little to dispel the fear that Johnson was not fully vested in the voting rights crusade.

Finally, just three days before the start of direct action in Selma, Johnson gave King the signal for which he had been waiting. During a January 15, 1965, telephone conversation, the President told King a voting rights bill was still very much in his plans. For the first time, Johnson also shared his anticipated approach with King, expressing his preference for a simple, straightforward bill advancing the premise that every person in the country has the right to vote when they reach a certain age. "We want to stand on a very clear principle," he said. "No special privileges, just equal opportunity for all."

As he had during their November meeting two months earlier, Johnson admitted to King that he wasn't ready to move yet but assured him that Attorney General Nicholas Katzenbach was researching the issue in preparation for drafting a bill. Mocking some of the more outrageous aspects of the Alabama literacy test, Johnson also said the legislation would prohibit tests "about what Chaucer said or Browning's poetry or memorizing constitutions or anything else." He suggested that King find the most outrageous example he could of someone being denied the right to vote and then repeat it continually during his public appearances. "If you can just take one instance and get it spread all over, that will help us shove it through in the end," he said.[2]

As usual, King was deferential in his comments to the President. He told Johnson he agreed with the strategy and thanked him for his efforts. But federal government support was just one of King's concerns as details of the Selma campaign were being finalized.

From the beginning, the ambitious voting rights campaign was complicated not just by white opposition or presidential politics but also by growing fissures within the civil rights movement itself. Never really a monolithic enterprise, the movement over the years had become even more fractious, attracting strong-willed leaders with a wide range of ideas, often conflicting, on how best to advance their cause.

As the movement grew and matured, its supporters had become more inclined to challenge old assumptions and practices. King and his associates in the SCLC remained committed to the practice of nonviolent protest, but other, typically younger, black leaders were growing frustrated with the slow pace of change. A riot at the end of the Birmingham campaign was the first troubling sign that not all protesters were committed to the nonviolence doctrine, a fear that reasserted itself when a four-day riot erupted in the Harlem area of New York City early in the summer of 1964.

Divisions were most noticeable between King's SCLC and the more aggressive Student Non-Violent Coordinating Committee (SNCC, commonly pronounced "snick"), and attempts to mesh their efforts frequently created suspicion and covert hostility. Though the two organizations shared the same goals, they had distinctly different operating philosophies. The SCLC relied primarily on King's star power to focus national attention on local conditions, while SNCC sought to develop leaders at the grassroots level instead of bringing them in from outside.[3]

SNCC members often felt over-worked and under-appreciated, and many grew contemptuous of the SCLC's emphasis on grand events and extensive media coverage. They felt, not without justification, that while they were doing the demanding, day-to-day organizational work, King and his associates were playing to the television cameras and taking credit for the movement's accomplishments. In response, SCLC leaders pointed to their undeniable record of success, and openly questioned SNCC's commitment to nonviolence, referencing comments made by Stokely Carmichael, a SNCC organizer, suggesting that blacks at some point would have to take up arms against their white oppressors.

The two organizations had similar roots, both springing from isolated protests in the late 1950s and early 1960s. The Southern Christian Leadership Conference was initially conceived by long-time King advisor Dr. Bayard Rustin of New York in the wake of the 1957 Montgomery bus boycott. Rustin's idea was to create an organization devoted to ending busing discrimination across the entire South through direct, nonviolent action. After a series of meetings, King was chosen to head the nonprofit organization. Others who played a key role in formation of the SCLC, in addition to Rustin, were Rev. Fred Shuttlesworth of Birmingham, Rev. Joseph Lowery of Mobile, Rev. Ralph Abernathy of Montgomery and Rev. C. K. Steele of Tallahassee. A small office was opened on Auburn Avenue in Atlanta with Ella Baker as SCLC's first — and for a long time, only — staff member.

Propelled by King's emerging public profile and incomparable rhetorical skills, the SCLC shot to the forefront of the civil rights movement, promoting a message of change through nonviolent protest as championed by Gandhi. King, who quickly became the face of the movement, never wavered from the Gandhian vision of change through peaceful means. Like Gandhi, he was a shrewd, tireless and efficient organizer who combined optimism with unshakeable determination.[4]

Much as the Montgomery bus boycott led to formation of the SCLC, the organizers of SNCC were inspired by an incident that occurred on February 1, 1960. On that date, a group of black college students from North Carolina A&T University refused to leave a Woolworth's lunch counter in Greensboro, where they had been denied service. The students were taunted and attacked by an angry white mob, and the resulting publicity sparked an ensuing wave of sit-ins in college towns across the South.

SNCC was created on the campus of Shaw University in Raleigh two months later to coordinate similar protests. Early leaders included future Georgia Congressman John Lewis, future Washington, D. C., Mayor Marion Barry, and future NAACP Director Julian Bond.

From the beginning, SNCC rejected high-profile events in favor of low-key grassroots projects aimed at improving individual communities. And in a departure from the SCLC's top-down management structure, in which King was the ultimate decision-maker, SNCC was a much more egalitarian organization that prided itself on making decisions by consensus.

Preceding both the SCLC and SNCC was the Congress of Racial Equality (CORE), which was founded as the Committee of Racial Equality in 1942 by an interracial group of students in Chicago but was largely ineffective during its early years. Like the SCLC, CORE was heavily influenced by Gandhi's pacifist teachings.

And then, of course, there was the venerable National Association for the Advancement of Colored People (NAACP). Founded in 1909, the NAACP was the oldest and most conservative civil rights organization in the country. Whereas the upstarts sought to advance their cause through protests and other forms of direct action, the NAACP worked primarily through official channels, relying on litigation and legislation, thus acquiring a reputation of being stodgy and out of step with the times.

For years, the major civil rights organizations co-existed peacefully, if not always harmoniously. By the mid-60s, however, things were changing. Angry over the exceedingly slow pace of change, younger members of SNCC and CORE, which had revitalized itself after years of dormancy, were increasingly militant and critical of the SCLC's strict adherence to nonviolent protest. Internal differences were becoming more visible to outsiders, and those who would challenge King's influence were growing more emboldened.

At this point, at least, the differences were more tactical than strategic. King's SCLC goals of equal rights and social justice were the same as those of SNCC and other more assertive organizations, but his approach was more moderate, and he typically remained open to negotiated solutions. By embracing moderation, King was better positioned to deal with white power brokers, telling them, in effect, if you don't bargain with me, you'll have to deal with SNCC or Malcolm X.

Historian August Meier aptly notes that King occupied the "vital center" of the civil rights movement, a position from which he could keep his coalition together by restraining the rash youths who formed the cutting edge of the movement, while at the same time admonishing the more conservative laggards to pick up their pace. In that sense, Meier says, King could be considered a "conservative militant."[5]

It was a difficult balancing act, but it worked. Given all the potential pitfalls, in fact, it worked surprisingly well. Never in U.S. history had a social movement been constructed from people of both genders and both races with such disparate backgrounds, socioeconomic standings, religions, occupations, and political philosophies.

That King could keep such a diverse collection of organizations and strong-willed people moving steadily in the same direction, unified if not always in precise accord, was a testament to his leadership abilities. Black Selma attorney J. L. Chestnut, who attended many contentious strategy sessions with King and his followers, grew to respect the SCLC leader as "one hell of a field general."[5]

Said Chestnut, in typically blunt fashion: "No one else could have unified the collection of ministers, gangsters, self-seekers, students, prima donnas and devoted, high-minded people we had in Selma that winter."[6]

Years later, Andrew Young characterized the relationship between SNCC and the SCLC as being "sort of like me and my younger brother," explaining, "We loved each other, but we fought all the time." Key to the relationship, Young said, was whether the individual SNCC members involved at any given time resented King's prominence. But, he added, "We never asked people whether they were SCLC people or SNCC people or NAACP people. We just brought people together."[7]

The Selma campaign would stretch that premise to the breaking point.

Chapter 3: The Selma campaign

By 1965, the Student Nonviolent Coordinating Committee was already active in Selma and the rest of Dallas County, having inaugurated a voter education project and mounted a drive to register black voters two years earlier. Bernard Lafayette, a young black divinity student and former Freedom Rider, was given control of SNCC's Selma project in February 1963, despite, or perhaps because of, his inexperience in field organization.

Essentially, Lafayette was assigned to Selma because nobody else wanted it. Due to its central location in the part of Alabama with the highest percentage of black residents, Selma previously had been investigated as a possible SNCC campaign site, but reports from that visit were discouraging: Selma whites had a firm grip on the levers of power. Blacks there were fearful and easily intimidated. Chances for a successful campaign were minimal.

But while young and inexperienced, Layfayette wasn't naïve. He was aware of the challenge that lay ahead. Years later, he recalled:

"I'd actually heard about Selma before [deciding to work there]. It was during the Freedom Rides when the bus I was

riding ... was stopped by state police who said it needed to take another route ... because there was a white mob waiting in Selma and they couldn't protect us. I'm saying to myself, 'Oh Lord — even the State Troopers are scared of that city.'"[1]

Selma is located in the Alabama "Black Belt," so named for its dark, fertile soil, not the bulk of its population. The Black Belt, which stretches across the mid-section of Alabama from the Chattahoochee River in the East westward to Mississippi, encompasses 15-20 counties, depending on the definition. The overwhelmingly rural area is dominated by mostly flat terrain interspersed with low, rolling hills. Small towns, many little more than a country crossroads, dot the map.

Historically, the city had special significance for both whites and blacks. An important manufacturing center of ammunition during the Civil War, Selma had been plundered by Northern troops a century earlier, an occurrence that still resonated with the white populace. The town had been burned, horses were butchered, and a number of women were attacked.

Following the war, Selma gained notoriety as the sometime home of Confederate General Nathan Forrest, the founder of the Ku Klux Klan, and the home of Alabama's first White Citizen's Council.

Blacks, meanwhile, considered Selma an intellectual, cultural and religious center. In 1965, the city was home to two small church-affiliated black colleges, Selma University, which was founded by the Alabama Colored Baptist Convention in 1878 to train ministers and Christian teachers, and Lutheran College. Both served Selma and adjoining counties to the west and south.[2]

Following decades of steady growth, Selma's population in 1965 was about 28,000, easily making it the largest city in the Black Belt. In fact, Selma was twice the size of the next largest city in the region, Tuskegee.

Then, as now, Selma's most prominent physical feature was the Edmund Pettus Bridge, which carries Highway 80 across the Alabama River. Built in 1940, the bridge was named for Edmund Winston Pettus, a former Confederate brigadier general and U.S. senator from Alabama. The imposing structure would soon become one of the most recognizable landmarks of the civil rights era.

Racially, the city was a virtual draw, half white and half black, but equality in numbers did not translate into equality of opportunity. Once the largest slave purchasing and deployment center in the area, Selma had a legacy of racism based on the entrenched belief that black residents were unfit to share power of any sort with their white neighbors.

White Selma thus controlled the city, both politically and economically, relegating most of the area's black residents to lives of grinding poverty, inadequate health care and the daily indignities visited upon them by Jim Crow-era segregation. Many of the city's black residents, the majority of whom worked in spirit-draining sharecropping arrangements, saw no way out of the dilemma and had succumbed to the belief that circumstances were unlikely to change regardless of what they did.

These black residents lacked hope and didn't want to risk what little they already had in terms of income and personal possessions by upsetting their white overseers. In fact, some movement leaders claimed it was more difficult and discouraging to argue oppression with black people than it was with whites.

Soon after his arrival in Selma, Lafayette, a handsome, unassuming young man who preferred suits and bow ties over the less formal dress of his colleagues, determined that SNCC's assessment of the city's racial dynamic was accurate. Despite a few committed members of the Dallas County Voters League, Selma's black population was non-committal at best and highly skeptical at worst. Lafayette concluded that his first struggle would be against black fear, not white resistance.[3]

Lafayette worked hard, often putting in 18-hour days, but the opposition was formidable, both from white citizens and blacks unwilling to risk the welfare of their families. "The Freedom Rider," as he became known, even had trouble finding a place to live and a church where he could hold mass meetings.

In one especially dispiriting meeting, recounted by attorney Chestnut, the head of the city's alliance of black ministers declared that Selma didn't have any racial problems. "We know how to get what we want from white people," the minister said. "You just have to know how to ask." To the laughter of others, the minister fell to his knees and held out his hat.[4]

That story is emblematic of the power disparity in Selma during the mid-60s. The city's black organizations remained mostly silent as whites adopted hard-line policies on issues of race, including voting rights. With the exception of the small and mostly ineffective Voters League, no one was even trying to organize blacks to pursue a goal beyond trying to get to heaven.

There were individual exceptions, of course. Chestnut, who played a key behind-the-scenes role in Selma as a lawyer for the Legal Defense Fund and unofficial advisor to King, recounts the efforts of one early activist in his book, "Black in Selma." Chestnut tells the story of Marie Foster, a widow with three children, who worked as a dental hygienist for her brother. For years, Foster took the literacy test, but according to the rejection notice, always "failed one or more pertinent questions." But Foster never gave up and always had a new plan for the Voters League about how to increase registration:

Said Chesnut:

> *"The Voters League had copies of the tests, which were changed monthly. Marie thought if the league sponsored a series of citizenship classes where people could see the tests and practice taking them, they'd be more willing to go to the courthouse and give it a try. We all said 'great idea', when she proposed this at a league meeting. The next Sunday, she went around to all the major black churches in Dallas County to announce the first class – and exactly one person showed up. He was an old man, Major Washington, who couldn't read or write. It is an example of Marie's indomitable spirit that she stayed with him until 10 o'clock, taught him to write his name, and continued to hold classes."*[5]

But the Marie Fosters of Selma were the exception. And even with a largely pliant black population, white Selma was vigilant in rooting out any threats to the status quo. As Lafayette had been warned – and as King would soon discover -- Selma presented an extraordinarily challenging environment.

On the night civil rights activist Medgar Evers was killed in Jackson, Mississippi, Bernard Lafayette almost met the same fate in Selma. Returning home from a mass meeting on June 14, 1963, he was approached by a white man who asked for help starting his stalled car. When Lafayette bent over the car to see what was wrong, the man clubbed him with the butt of a gun. Lafayette crumpled to the street and then struggled to his feet. Lafayette's nonviolence training kicked in, and he refused to respond to the attack. He observed his assailant silently, but didn't make a move. The man hit him again and again. Each time, Lafayette would stand up, blood dripping down on his shirt, and silently face the attacker.

Rattled by this unexpected behavior, the assailant backed away, got into his car and fled. Relating this story years later, Lafayette said, "Unexpected behavior sometimes can have the impact of arresting the conscience of your assailant, because they don't know how to respond to you. They expect you to run, they expect you to plead for your life, they expect you to fight back. I did none of those things; as I was trained in the movement, I simply confronted him and looked at him. That upset him, unnerved him."[6]

Lafayette survived that encounter, which was later determined to be part of a Klan-inspired plot to kill civil rights leaders in Alabama, Mississippi and Louisiana, but the SNCC voter registration drive was sputtering. The combination of a hostile and entrenched white power structure and a cowed and indifferent black community was not the formula for a successful movement. Still, Lafayette and his dedicated volunteers soldiered on, content to claim small victories while taking their defeats in stride.

But white supremacists were happy with the status quo in Selma and were not going to relinquish it without a fight. So oblivious were many white residents to the private suffering of the city's black residents, that many didn't even know why these activists were causing such a fuss.

As Andrew Young said years later:

> *"In those early days of 1965, the white townspeople of Selma looked at us not only through eyes of hatred, but with minds and spirit that failed to comprehend in the least why we were there. Selma was symbolic of race relations in any small Southern town trapped in a time warp; we could have*

chosen any of a hundred similar towns, but we could not have found a more exemplary case of social polarity of a more abused and oppressed black community."[7]

Indeed, it is said that Selma was to Alabama what Greenwood was to Mississippi: a town where "almost every element of white resistance is present ... in magnified form."[8]

But despite the obvious dangers, the city also had a lot to recommend it as an SCLC campaign site: Many of the local white leaders were unreasonable and thus more inclined to force a showdown; the local black churches, while not yet engaged, were powerful institutions; black residents clearly demonstrated their need for help on the voting issue; and, logistically, the city itself was a reasonable distance from SCLC headquarters in Atlanta.

In addition, the area was well-known to many of the key players. King's wife, Coretta Scott King, was from nearby Marion; Young had served at the Congregational Church in Marion a decade earlier and had his first date with his future wife in Selma; and Abernathy, King's right-hand man, was born and raised in Hopewell, Alabama, and went to college at Alabama State University in Montgomery.

Most importantly, King, despite his familiarity with the city and its potential pitfalls, was intrigued by the notion of taking a stand in the midst of one of the most virulent anti-black areas of the country. His interest – indeed, his fundamental philosophy --ran counter to the preferences of the NAACP, which consistently argued that the movement should establish momentum by concentrating on easier targets.[9]

Once the SCLC started focusing on the possibilities of Selma as the site for a voter rights drive, there was a certain inevitability to the final decision, and on the final day of

1964, the Alabama field staff joined Bevel in Selma to plan the campaign launch.

Though their organizing efforts had met with little success, Lafayette and his SNCC colleagues were nonetheless dismayed when King and his entourage descended on the city just two days later.

Chairman John Lewis expressed SNCC's unhappiness with the SCLC's perceived intrusion. It was, he said, the same old story. "We dug in early, did the groundwork, laid the foundation, then the SCLC came in with their headline-grabbing, hit-and-run tactics, doing nothing to nurture local leaders but instead bringing in their own leaders, then leaving after they had gotten what they needed out of it."[10]

But Lewis, a remarkably mature and earnest young man, who, like Young, always put the good of the movement ahead of personal politics, wasn't totally opposed to the SCLC intervention. He knew his colleagues felt they were being shoved aside by the King organization's juggernaut, but he also had a sincere respect and admiration for what the SCLC was trying to accomplish. SNCC, Lewis concluded, would have to be satisfied with its new role as junior partner in Selma.

Lewis was born and raised on a farm near Troy, Alabama, a rural hamlet some 100 miles southeast of Selma, and attended college at the American Baptist Theological Seminary in Nashville, a tiny school for black ministerial candidates. It was there that Lewis met future movement leaders James Lawson, James Bevel, Diane Nash, and Lafayette, and immersed himself in the history and philosophy of nonviolent protest.

His first direct action as part of the movement came in mid-February 1960, when he and a group of colleagues attempted to integrate a whites-only lunch counter at the Woolworth's Store in downtown Nashville.

Short of stature but long on ideals, Lewis was serious, sensitive, and a self-described "square." Not surprisingly, he frequently found himself in the role of peacemaker during the Selma campaign. Although his heart was with SNCC, Lewis never lost sight of the larger picture and thus was willing to tolerate many of the SCLC's operational idiosyncrasies and over-sized egos if doing so would help the campaign. He also had great respect for King, in later years referring to him as "my friend, my brother, my inspiration."

Sensitive to the charged political situation, King's associates insisted they were not trying to undermine SNCC's efforts but were merely trying to help. "The local black leadership in

Selma was really responsible for the Selma movement," said Young, who had recently been appointed executive director of the SCLC. "Selma was not a place that we picked out. We did not choose them. They chose us."[11]

Technically, that was correct. The Dallas County Voters League, which was in effect a branch of the NAACP, had in fact issued a cry for help. But the decision to go to Selma was not an altruistic response to that appeal. It was a calculated decision based on what the SCLC believed would best serve its national interests, which, to be fair, would also serve the interests of Selma's black residents.

The site thus determined, King needed to establish a campaign command structure. He named Young overall coordinator and chose three of his key lieutenants, James Bevel, Albert Turner, and Hosea Williams, to run field projects in Selma and neighboring communities,

Young, who would subsequently go on to serve as U.N. ambassador, Georgia congressman and mayor of Atlanta, was indispensable as King's voice of reason. Self-effacing and loyal to a fault, he had the ability to focus on the issues at hand without being distracted by the internal drama and bickering that so often beset the civil rights movement.

Young had left a promising career with the National Council of Churches in New York in 1961 to focus his energy on the southern civil rights movement, enticed, he says, by "a new wind of freedom for people of color." Inspired by news of sit-ins and other forms of protest emanating from the South, Young settled in Dorchester, Georgia, where he coordinated community citizenship programs, responsibility for which was subsequently transferred from the United Church of Christ to King's fledgling SCLC. He would remain with King for the duration.

These were some of King's best people. And while the Selma campaign was ostensibly a joint effort involving the SCLC, SNCC, and the Voters League, there was no doubt about which organization would be in charge.

King was taking a calculated risk by giving three forceful personalities operational responsibility for the Selma campaign, especially Bevel and Williams, each of whom felt the other was a menace to the movement. Bevel was ideologically pure to a fault, while Williams could be abrasive and confrontational. Though ostensibly on the same team, tension between the two was palpable, and both were prone to letting personal competition and strategic differences interfere with the goals of the movement.[12]

King was aware of these clashing egos but actually considered it helpful to the campaign, reasoning that "you need some folks like Hosea and Bevel who are crazy enough to take on anything and anybody." He also knew that both men – all three, including Turner -- had a remarkably unselfish commitment to the cause of civil rights, despite their personal and philosophical differences.[13]

For their part, the three veteran campaign leaders knew what they were up against, but embraced the challenge.

Bevel in particular was fascinated with Selma. Mostly, he liked it because the town had so little use for racial gamesmanship. White Selma and black Selma could not have been more divided. White residents didn't try to mask their true feelings, as they had begun to do in other communities, and black residents knew right where they stood. But whereas Bevel found that crude sense of honesty intriguing, others were less enamored, fearing that what made Selma a logical campaign target also made it infinitely more dangerous. To these movement leaders, Selma was not so much a town as a hick community run by angry and dedicated segregationists determined to cling to the past.[14]

Bevel wasn't worried. By now an experienced veteran of many campaigns, he was confident in his understanding of the nonviolence philosophy and his ability to translate it into action. Within a few days, he had recruited about 100 volunteers to be divided between five city wards.

King had a great deal of respect for Bevel's intellect and passion. Though he remained wary of the young man's unpredictable nature and penchant for philosophical moralizing, he trusted Bevel to get results.[15]

In 1963, as Alabama project director for the SCLC, Bevel persuaded King to allow children to participate in anti-segregation demonstrations in Birmingham, in which they would almost surely face arrest. King had deep misgivings about this approach but finally agreed. The demonstrations early that year overwhelmed the city, and many Americans were horrified by televised images of black children being arrested or soaked and bowled over by law enforcement officers wielding powerful fire hoses. The resulting publicity helped turn the campaign in King's favor and ultimately led to a decisive victory.

The charismatic Bevel was both passionate and peculiar. He often wore overalls over a shirt and tie; he shaved his head and sometimes covered it with a yarmulke in honor of Old Testament prophets. Many people found him interesting, others just thought he was strange.

Not surprisingly, white Selma residents quickly developed an especially profound dislike of Bevel. Whereas SNCC's Lafayette had deliberately kept a low profile in Selma, Bevel did not. It might have been his colorful dress; his high profile around town; or, most likely, his confident, self-assured manner, but Bevel seemed to irritate the segregationists more than any of the other black leaders.

Conversely, many of Selma's black residents appreciated the SCLC's efforts and admired Bevel's style, albeit quietly. Most were resigned to the belief that white power was invincible, that they might make some minor advances but would never match whites in terms of voting numbers or ability to affect public policy. They thus were reluctant to publicly align themselves with the SCLC movement.

As King saw it, this pattern of so-called "black denial," especially as it pertained to voting rights, stemmed from four main roadblocks:

- A "Gestapo-like" control of county and local government by men of power and brutality that produced a fear rooted in feelings of inferiority.
- City ordinances and local laws that allowed authorities to monitor and harass blacks trying to devise a group plan of action.
- The slow pace of the registrar and limited number of days and hours in which the office was open.
- The literacy tests, which were routinely administered unfairly.[16]

He said: "Clearly, the heart of the voting problem lay in the fact that the machinery for enforcing this basic right was in the hands of state-appointed officials answerable to the very people who believed they could continue to wield power in the South only so long as the Negro was disenfranchised."[17]

As a result, black voting in the mid-60s was almost non-existent in Selma. While 67 percent of Selma's voter-age white residents were registered; just over 2 percent of the 15,000 black voters – 325 – were registered.

King and his associates were determined to change those numbers, but they first had to galvanize the oppressed and beleaguered black community in Selma and neighboring communities.

It would not be an easy task. Heading the opposition was a law enforcement officer who armed his deputies with billy clubs and cattle prods, and was infuriated when anyone defied his authority.

Chapter 4: Identifying the Villain

Dallas County Sheriff Jim Clark was an imposing figure. Tall and beefy with a seemingly permanent scowl, Clark wasted little time on community relations or diplomatic niceties. His supporters called him a no-nonsense law and order man, old-school but effective; his critics called him crazy.

Clark, 43, was a polarizing figure with a hair-trigger temper. His intense dislike of African-Americans and inability to ignore any personal criticism or perceived threat to the established social order reminded many civil rights activists of another infamous Alabama lawman, Birmingham Public Safety Commissioner Eugene "Bull" Connor, he of the snarling police dogs and high-pressure fire hoses.

Like Connor, Clark had little regard for the First Amendment rights of free speech and peaceful assembly, at least insofar as they applied to his efforts to keep Dallas County's black residents in their place, which he considered his sworn duty. He was rarely without his anti-integration lapel badge, which read, "Never." Also like Connor, he took any criticism of his tactics as a personal affront and would often react violently when challenged.

Clark might have been a madman, but movement leaders hoped they could use that to their advantage. They feared Clark, but they also needed him. Indeed, civil rights campaigns over the years had proven that an identifiable "villain" was necessary for success. The most successful protests – most notably, Birmingham – were those in which the image of nonviolent African-Americans peacefully seeking to secure their basic civil rights could be presented alongside a morally bankrupt white power structure determined to keep the protesters under foot whatever the cost. The best-case scenario for the movement was when an easily manipulated individual would emerge as the embodiment of that power structure.

And therein lay the great paradox of the nonviolent protest movement. To be successful – to ensure that the rest of America would pay attention – King and his colleagues not only had to accept the possibility of violence, they sometimes had to instigate it. Without dramatic news coverage, the movement would be powerless, and without violent confrontation, there would be no dramatic news coverage.

Critics argue that King deliberately sought to provoke violence, which is why his campaigns focused on extreme white supremacist communities instead of the South's more racially progressive areas. The NAACP constantly urged King to concentrate on cities where the battle was already half won -- places such as Mobile, Atlanta and Nashville -- instead of risking confrontation in less enlightened locales. But King believed that dramatic confrontation offered the fastest path to federal legislation.

Understandably, this was a sensitive topic. The leader of a massive nonviolent protest movement could not be seen as someone who actually encouraged violence, and the SCLC was frequently forced to explain this apparent dichotomy.[1]

King and his associates consistently denied courting violence, insisting that their goal was to put so many people in jail that the system would crash, not to provoke racist retaliation. To blame peaceful demonstrators for the violence they encountered, King argued, would be like "condemning the robbed man because his possession of money precipitated the evil act of robbery."[2]

Young was more direct, contending that the movement did not cause problems in Selma, but rather brought them to the surface where they could be addressed. He said: "Sheriff Clark has been beating black heads in the back of the jail for years, and we're only saying to him that if he still wants to beat heads, he'll have to do it on Main Street, at noon, in front of CBS, NBC, and ABC television cameras."[3]

Author David Garrow contends that the SCLC's strategy bordered on "nonviolent provocation," a characterization that seems reasonable, but was rejected by movement leaders.

"That," Young said, referring to the notion of provocation, "was not an SCLC plan. What we did say was that we would put so many people in jail that we would bring the system to a halt and that our emphasis was on noncooperation and economic withdrawal."[4]

Perhaps so, but even those who feared Clark the most acknowledged that his mercurial personality and unwitting willingness to play the villain might be just what was needed to re-energize a flagging movement that peaked with the July 2 signing of the 1964 Civil Rights Act, but had been meandering ever since.

Thanks to the 1964 legislation, Jim Crow, shorthand for the assortment of discriminatory laws and practices adopted by many southern states at the end of Reconstruction in 1877 to impose restrictions on black residents, was already on the run. Jim Crow laws, such as those that provided for separate public facilities and forbade black and white marriages, were federally sanctioned by the infamous *Plessy v. Ferguson* Supreme Court ruling of 1896 and remained lawful for nearly 60 years. Now considered one of the most shameful rulings in the court's history, *Plessy* decreed that "separate but equal" accommodations were allowable under the Constitution.

In 1954, the Court overturned *Plessy*, in *Brown v. Board of Education*, the landmark case that eliminated the constitutional basis for segregation. And even though it would take years of legislation and legal maneuvering for the federal government to begin chipping away at Jim Crow, changes were beginning to occur across the South.

By 1963, the fluttering winds of freedom gave rise to a mood of cautious optimism, highlighted by the famous march on Washington, and captured perfectly by Sam Cooke, who sang:

> *"Oh there been times that I thought it couldn't last for long*
> *"But now I think I'm able to carry on*
> *"It's been a long time coming*
> *"But I know a change is gonna come"*

But Jim Crow was more than a set of laws. It was an unspoken code of racial customs and taboos that reflected the South's enduring reluctance to embrace integration. And even nearly 10 years after the *Brown* decision, the core of that code remained impervious to attempts at truly substantive change.

To the hard-eyed realists at the SCLC, the incremental steps forward were, at best, too little, too late and, at worst, ephemeral changes that would actually prove counterproductive by cloaking the need for comprehensive and enforceable reform.

White segregationists had begun yielding on demands for open lunch counters and better seating on buses not only because the economic consequences were relatively small but also because they knew they could easily devise ways to circumvent the spirit of those concessions, especially after the protesters and television cameras left town.

King and his colleagues understood as much, which is why they were pushing so hard for a comprehensive voting rights bill. Said Young: "Focusing on public accommodations in Birmingham had helped bring about a very comprehensive civil rights bill. Unfortunately, though the bill gave black citizens the right of access to public accommodations, it did not protect their voting rights, a forum in which they might actually help change the laws that kept them down."[5]

Movement leaders were determined to secure black voting rights even if it meant bloodshed. White opponents, sensing a direct threat to the political system they had dominated for more than 100 years, had proved that they would kill to protect their way of life and there was no reason to think they wouldn't do it again.

Such was the situation King faced when he officially announced the Selma campaign on January 2, 1965, by addressing a packed house at the Brown AME Church, an old-fashioned red-brick building in the midst of a black neighborhood on Sylvan Street that quickly became the campaign's primary headquarters. The meeting was held in defiance of an injunction ordered by Circuit Judge James Hare on July 9, 1964, essentially prohibiting the city's black residents from congregating in small groups, and served notice that the protesters would not be easily intimidated.

Hare's injunction prohibited 50 specifically named blacks and 15 black organizations from holding public meetings of more than 3 people. It was drafted in response to what he considered an ominous rash of incidents in which Selma blacks were testing their new-found liberties under the recently enacted Civil Rights Act. On Saturday, July 4, 1964, four black volunteers of SNCC's Selma Literacy Project tested the new law by visiting the Thirsty Boy drive-in. A crowd of whites attacked them, and the black volunteers were arrested for trespassing. And at the city's movie theater, black students came down from the "Colored" balcony to the white-only main floor. They too were beaten, and police officers ordered the theater closed.

The injunction was clearly unconstitutional, but Hare was a man of immense power in Selma, and one did not challenge his rulings capriciously. He was no doubt aware that his injunction could not pass constitutional muster, but was convinced that "drastic situations call for drastic solutions."[6]

A committed, old-school segregationist, Hare was passive and tolerant of blacks, so long as they remained quiet and obedient. He fancied himself an intellectual and an expert on the tribes of Africa. Extensive study, he claimed, gave him the ability to determine the tribes from which local blacks descended, as well as the typical personal characteristics of those tribe members. Hare often said that the problem in Dallas County was that most of its blacks came from two of Africa's least-productive tribes, the Ibos and Congolese. "We just got a bad boatload of slaves," he would lament, shaking his head.[7]

Sheriff Clark was generally thought to get his marching orders from Hare, who, in turn, followed the lead of Gov. George Wallace and State Safety Commissioner Al Lingo. Together, they wielded an inordinate amount of power across the region.

Of that mix, the relationship between Clark and Hare was the most significant to Selma residents, and at times it seemed as much social as professional. In a very real sense, Hare was a mid-1900s version of a mid-1800s plantation master, and Clark was his overseer, the man who ran the plantation and kept the blacks in line. Clark enjoyed his power, but Hare never let him forget who was boss, as well as who bested whom on the social ladder. He was notoriously adept at manipulating Clark, who typically would respond to the judge's demands with a meek "Yessir."[8]

Clark added his own violent touches to the judge's tactical plans, but Hare was the real power behind white Selma's response to the black threat and was confident of his ability to suppress it before it grew out of control.

However, things were beginning to change in Selma's black community, and the huge turnout at Brown Chapel on Sunday night served notice that the protesters would not be so easily intimidated this time, injunction or not. Eager to see the man they had heard so much about, some 700 people braved a rare Selma snowstorm to squeeze into the church and hear King deliver a rousing address that was half speech, half sermon. His goal was to encourage a mostly frightened and apathetic black community to stand up for itself. Police were present but only to control traffic, not to make arrests.[9]

King gave the audience a version of his famous "Give Us the Ballot" speech first delivered at his 1957 Prayer Pilgrimage March on Washington. In it, he cites the positive changes that would occur when blacks were granted unfettered access to the polls. Give us the ballot, he said, and:

- we will no longer have to worry the federal government about our basic rights ...
- we will no longer plead to the federal government for passage of an anti-lynching law ...
- we will fill our legislative halls with men of good will ...
- we will place judges on the benches of the South who will do justly and love mercy ...
- we will quietly and nonviolently, without rancor or bitterness, implement the Supreme Court's decision of May 17, 1954. (Brown v. Board of Education)

King told the large crowd, "We will seek to arouse the federal government by marching by the thousand," and added for emphasis, "We must be willing to go to jail by the thousands." The frenzied crowd responded with calls of "Amen" and "Give us the ballot."[10]

King's address was effective in persuading many local black residents, especially the black professional class, to get personally involved. Even many of those who had held back for fear of losing their jobs or being jailed were moved to action. King's inspirational message gave them the courage needed to put concerns about their personal livelihoods aside for the greater good.

King announced that the marches would not begin for several weeks, giving campaign leaders time to organize, and outlined the plan that would be followed if, as expected, county registrars refused to register black voters: The organization would first appeal to Gov. Wallace and then to the state legislature. If and when those appeals were rejected, they would go to Washington and seek support from Congress.[11]

King did not get a chance to size up Clark, his anticipated adversary, during this initial visit. The sheriff was in Miami, watching as No. 1 ranked Alabama fell to Texas in the first night game in Orange Bowl history. The Alabama quarterback was a charismatic young man named Joe Namath.

******

Over the next few weeks, Selma's black community crackled with energy and excitement as SCLC and SNCC workers held evening rallies to gather support for the cause. Their followers were urged to be courageous in the face of white intimidation, and were given a crash course in the theory and techniques of nonviolent protest. They learned the philosophy and history of nonviolence and were taught how to disregard taunts and physical threats. Organizers showed them how to let their bodies go limp when they were being forcibly moved. They were instructed to carry moist handkerchiefs for use in the event of a tear-gas attack.

Two weeks didn't allow much time for all the recruiting, training, and planning that had to be done, but King and his colleagues, fearful of losing the sense of purpose they had created, wanted to move quickly.

By Tuesday, January 12, block captains had been elected for each city ward. Using an interorganizational approach, staff members canvassed the wards in pairs, one from the SCLC and one from SNCC. Bernard Lafayette, who had arrived from Chicago to promote cooperation, approved the tandem approach.[12]

Soon, the planning was over and it was time to act. Still unsure of the campaign's readiness, King and his top advisors nevertheless decided that it would be riskier to wait than to move.

Direct action began January 18 when King and SNCC leader Lewis led 400 eager marchers to the Dallas County Courthouse. Sheriff Clark was there to greet them, standing at the courthouse entrance with arms folded across his chest and a scowl on his face in an obvious attempt to emulate Gov. Wallace. Hecklers from the American Nazi Party stood by, but there was no violence.

As the TV cameras rolled, Clark stepped forward and announced there were too many marchers to enter the courthouse. He ordered them into the alley to wait while registrars called in prospective voters one at a time. The protesters knew Clark was stalling but decided to play along. Reluctantly, they allowed themselves to be herded into the alley, where they milled around for a few hours before breaking off for the day.

Given the weeks of buildup, it was an anti-climactic day for the marchers, many of whom appeared dispirited when they left. King and his lieutenants knew they let themselves be led into the alley too easily. They also knew that Clark had won the day's public relations battle. Because he had maintained his composure, the sheriff was viewed as firm yet accommodating by television audiences who had not yet seen the kind of vicious brutality of which he was capable.

Disappointed that nothing had happened to call attention to their cause, rally leaders held a lengthy meeting to consider various options. The mood was somber, but no one was ready to concede defeat after a single day. The group instead decided on a change in tactics. When ordered into the alley the next day, they would refuse to leave the sidewalk in front of the courthouse.[13]

The hope, of course, was that Clark would retaliate. If he did not, the SCLC was prepared to pick another target, with the likely choice being Marion, the seat of nearby Perry County.

Meanwhile, Selma's new mayor, a young man named Joseph Smitherman, was cautiously optimistic following the uneventful first day. Smitherman, 34, was an appliance salesman with no prior experience in municipal government. A slight, wiry man with jug-handle ears, Smitherman was not part of Selma's white establishment. In fact, he had more in common with many Selma blacks than with the city's bluebloods. Smitherman had no college education and lived in an older home in a run-down neighborhood. His widowed mother was on welfare.[14]

Smitherman had run for office in hopes of improving the city's economic condition and routine services such as trash collection and park maintenance, but now found himself in the midst of a complex civil rights dispute that would challenge even the most experienced public servant. The new mayor had appealed in vain to black community leaders to try to keep King out of the city by promising to pave roads in predominantly black areas of the city, which were mostly dirt.

Now that King's presence was a reality, however, he was convinced that a reasoned, low-key approach was the only way to defuse what was otherwise likely to be a series of contentious confrontations that would damage the city's reputation. Smitherman was prepared to wait out the marchers in hopes that they would soon lose interest. However, he was also tugged in the other direction by members of the white underclass from which he had come. Those folks believed the black rebellion had to be quashed, by force if unnecessary.

Shortly after his election, Smitherman had appointed a knowledgeable and moderate man, Wilson Baker, as public safety director with authority over all law enforcement in the city except for Clark's jurisdiction in and around the county courthouse. Baker was a former Selma police captain who had lost a race against Sheriff Clark in 1958 and gone on to teach criminology classes at the University of Alabama at Tuscaloosa. Even more so than Smitherman, Baker believed that any violence or unnecessary force used against the protesters would be counterproductive to the city. He saw how the use of excessive force had damaged Birmingham's reputation and was determined to avoid a similar outcome.

Baker was smarter than Clark and much more aware of the power of public perceptions. If there can be such a thing, he was an *enlightened* racist, one who sought to keep blacks subservient while at the same time treating them courteously and respectfully. Smitherman hoped he would give Selma a more nuanced defense of segregation.

Most important to Smitherman, Baker possessed the self control that Clark lacked and was not likely to be goaded into an unwise use of force. His plan, developed in conjunction with Smitherman, was to minimize any move toward integration by offering a kinder and gentler form of resistance, one that wouldn't result in Page 1 photos in newspapers across the nation. "I'm not for integration," Baker once said. "But I can understand what they're doing and why. Hell, if I were a nigger I'd be right out there with them."[15]

Smitherman was confident of Baker's ability to handle the marchers with the required sensitivity and reasoned that if Clark restrained himself, the press would have no reason to remain in Selma. On this first test, at least, he prevailed. Day One was behind him without incident, and Smitherman allowed himself the hopeful thought that the Selma initiative would soon be history.

That, of course, was problematic for campaign leaders, who were seeking to generate a public backlash against Selma authorities. While Smitherman and Baker hoped to keep Clark under control, the SCLC was determined to provoke the quick-tempered sheriff into rash action that would illustrate what they were up against. The strategic standoff didn't last long -- one day, to be precise.

On January 19, the second day of the SCLC marches, Clark grew infuriated when the marchers refused to decamp to the alley. After the crowd had assembled, Clark strode forward and shouted, "All right. Y'all move into the alley now and we'll call your name when it's time to register." Refusing to budge, the marchers watched as Clark's face grew red and the muscles in his jaw tightened.

"I said, y'all move and move now!"[16]

Nothing.

His pride at stake, Clark exploded. He grabbed the first protester within reach, who happened to be prominent Selma civil rights leader Amelia Boynton, and roughly shoved her down the courthouse sidewalk to a waiting patrol car. Camera shutters clacked furiously.

Clark picked the wrong woman to mess with. Boynton, at age 54, had already devoted a good portion of her life to the civil rights movement, and was revered for her dedication to the cause. An elegant woman, Boynton was a veteran of early NAACP efforts and one of Selma's few registered black voters. She was not easily frightened. In addition to her efforts on behalf of voter registration, Boynton and her husband encouraged black residents to abandon sharecropping and go to work for themselves and their families. She and her husband were constantly threatened and told to leave town. "Boynton," angry whites would say, "if you keep taking the good niggers off the farm, we won't have anybody to work for us."[17]

Clearly, she would not be intimidated, not even by the menacing specter of a billy club-wielding Jim Clark. But Clark didn't know that, nor did he really care. His orders ignored, his authority challenged, Clark reverted to type, using brute force to regain the upper hand. It was a nasty scene, and movement leaders had trouble hiding their private elation behind their public protestations.

Clark insisted ludicrously that Boynton was telling the marchers to enter the courthouse offices, throw books on the floor, and urinate on the desks. "When she wouldn't leave the premises," he said, "I was forced to arrest her."[18]

Boynton contends her only sin was not moving fast enough when ordered by Clark to get back in line. "I would not get in the line," she said. "I let him pick me up off the ground by grabbing me and throwing me in the car."[19]

Boynton was the most prominent protester arrested that day but not the only one. Before the day was over, deputies had arrested some 60 demonstrators for defying Clark's order to move to the alley. The next day the New York Times and the Washington Post published photographs of the sheriff pushing Boynton down the street, billy club at the ready.

Smitherman and Baker were furious. Clark had taken the bait, and the movement had its villain.

Chapter 5: The protests

The battle now engaged, spirits were high at a Selma mass meeting the night of Amelia Boynton's arrest. To roars of approval from the large crowd, the Reverend Ralph Abernathy, the SCLC's second-in-command, recommended a new name for the conference's honorary membership roll – Sheriff Jim Clark. After all, Abernathy said, Clark had done more for the movement that day than anyone else in the city.[1]

Throughout the campaign, Abernathy's irreverent, good-natured humor would serve as a perfect counterpoint to King's more high-minded proclamations. Years together had given the top two SCLC officials a chance to develop an effective working relationship, and each trusted the other implicitly.

More arrests were made the next day, Wednesday, January 20, as Clark tried to herd the demonstrators to a side door away from the main courthouse entrance. Speaking quietly in an obvious attempt to stay calm, Clark said, "You got to move out of the way, so people can use the front door here."

On its face, it was not an unreasonable request, but the marchers saw it as just another delay tactic and attempt to minimize their visible presence. They were in no mood to comply and refused to move.

Clark's ruddy complexion deepened. "Arrest them," he shouted to his deputies as he turned to leave, disgusted.

Moments later, as the deputies began rounding up disobedient protesters, Wilson Baker arrived, hoping to forge a compromise. Baker said the demonstrators could remain in front of the building provided they keep a path open so people could go in and out. Baker had either forgotten or didn't care that he was now on Clark's turf but was quickly reminded who was in charge of the courthouse grounds.

From out of nowhere, Clark sprinted over. "No they can't!" he shouted, furious that Baker had intruded on his territory. The marchers watched in stunned silence as Clark and Baker faced off, their mutual animosity apparent to everyone.

Not surprisingly, Clark prevailed. Baker stood aside, and by the end of the day more than 200 arrests had been made. Equally important, movement participants had discovered that Clark and Baker hated each other at least as much as they hated the demonstrators.[2]

Clark and Baker not only had different beliefs and approaches to issues of race, they had different constituencies, which doubtless affected the way they conducted business. Clark's constituents were the many people scattered across Dallas County outside Selma city limits, many of whom were poor white farmers eager to preserve their tenuous rung on the socioeconomic ladder by thwarting any kind of black advancement. Baker, meanwhile, was beholden to the same group of people as Smitherman, businessmen interested in economic growth and an expanding tax base. These white residents were typically more "moderate" than their out-county brethren, some due to the altruistic belief that integration was a moral issue, but many others who considered it distasteful yet necessary for their own economic well-being.[3]

In another encouraging sign for protesters, the press was beginning to show more interest in the Selma campaign. The *New York Times* was in the process of expanding its civil rights coverage, and the Los Angeles Times sent award-winning reporter Jack Nelson, a native of Talladega, Alabama, to Selma. Nelson quickly discovered that his editors on the West Coast were not quite prepared for unvarnished southern coverage. According to "The Race Beat," a book by Gene Roberts and Herb Klibanoff, Nelson heard Clark order his deputies to "get those niggers off the courthouse steps" and quoted him precisely in his story. "You can't use the word 'nigger' in the *L.A. Times*," an editor told Nelson in an urgent phone call. " You mean that you want me to quote Jim Clark as saying, 'Get those KNEE-GROES off the courthouse steps?' " an astonished Nelson shot back. Nelson prevailed.[4]

Satisfied with the way things were going, King and Abernathy returned to Atlanta for a few days to tend to their own parishes and other SCLC business. Young, Bevel, and the others kept the pressure on during King's absence, and white Selma received a shock on Friday, January 22, when more than 100 black Selma school teachers marched to the courthouse, demanding to be registered. It was a significant development, especially given what these teachers were putting at risk.

Black teachers could be fired "at will" by all-white school boards, members of which were often eager to root out "agitators." In many parts of the South, membership in the NAACP or involvement in any form of civil rights activity – including trying to register to vote – was grounds for immediate dismissal.

But in Selma, a few school teachers, such as Margaret Moore and Rev. Frederick D. Reese defied the school board and Citizens Council by assuming leadership roles. As the Selma marches intensified and grew to include students, Reese, Moore, and a few others began organizing and mobilizing the black teachers. They challenged their apprehensive colleagues, *"How can we teach American civics if we ourselves cannot vote?"*

After school on January 22, the teachers gathered at Clark Elementary School, many dressed in their Sunday best — the women in hats, gloves, and high-heels; the men in dark suits. Silently, 110 teachers — almost every black teacher in Selma — marched to the courthouse. It was a seminal event. Nowhere in the South had teachers ever publicly marched *as* teachers.

Sheriff Clark and his ever-present posse were there to confront the teachers when they arrived at the courthouse. Despite pleas from the Selma School Board president and superintendent, the teachers attempted to enter the courthouse, only to be poked and shoved back down the steps by Clark and his crew.

"This courthouse is a serious place of business, and you seem to think you can take it just to be Disneyland on parade," Clark scolded. "Do you have business in the courthouse."

Reese responded, "The only business we have is to come to the Board of Registrars to register ..."

Clark cut him short. "You came down here to make a mockery out of this courthouse and we're not going to have it," he said.

The teachers tried again to enter the building, and again were repelled.

When the teachers approached a third time, Clark threatened to arrest them all but was persuaded to back off after conferring with several courthouse officials. Meanwhile, Andrew Young decided that the point had been made and called for the marchers to return to the school, where they were greeted by a throng of cheering students.[5]

The teacher march was problematic for Selma segregationists. The marchers could not be portrayed as outside agitators, nor could they be dismissed as local misfits or troublemakers. They were members of Selma's educated class, professional people who just happened to be black.

In the excitement of the moment, Andrew Young engaged in a bit of hyperbole, calling the teacher march "the most significant thing that has happened in the racial movement since Birmingham."[6]

Clark saw it differently. Years later, he told an interviewer that some of the teachers claimed they were told they had to march "or they would suffer for it." It was a bit of verbal jousting that would repeat itself frequently, the marchers exaggerating the impact of their efforts or the response to those efforts, and the white establishment contending that the good black people of Selma were being cynically exploited by professional agitators. Regardless, the SCLC campaign had given black Selma hope for the future and, as evidenced by the teachers march, a unified sense of purpose.

Marches and mass arrests in Selma continued throughout the next week. Spirits remained high, but the campaign was not yet resonating with the American people the way organizers had hoped. Clark continued to abuse his authority and delighted in making arrests, but there was a certain boring sameness to the proceedings, which were all played out against the same courthouse background. The fact that the confrontations were taking place on such a small stage seemed to diminish its visual impact. Television coverage was thorough, but the campaign appeared to be losing the sense of urgency it needed to succeed.

Young, Bevel, and the SCLC's Selma staff decided in late January that it was time to renew interest in the campaign by having King submit to intentional arrest. This tactic had worked well in Birmingham, and organizers hoped to duplicate its success in Selma.

King and Abernathy returned to Selma on Sunday, January 31, and during a late-night strategy session plans were made for King's arrest the following day. Several hundred volunteers showed up at Brown Chapel early Monday morning and were told that they would march en masse, not split into smaller groups as they had been doing to avoid Judge Hare's parade ordinance. The goal, King told them, was to get arrested.

The group left Brown and had proceeded no more than a few blocks before Wilson Baker brought the march to a halt and arrested 260 participants, including King and Abernathy. King and Abernathy refused to accept bail and were led away to a special cell, with King telling newsmen, "I must confess this is a deliberate attempt to dramatize conditions in this city, state and community."[7]

As anticipated, King's arrest galvanized the movement and aroused a sleepy press corps, sparking renewed interest in the campaign. Later that day, another large group of marchers was arrested outside the courthouse, and, for the first time, rumbles were being heard in one of the area's outlying communities, as SCLC staffers led hundreds of Perry County residents in a protest march in Marion.

By now, some 3,000 protesters had been arrested, and as the Selma jail cells quickly filled to capacity and beyond, prisoners were transferred to jails in other counties or stashed in work camps and a variety of makeshift jails across the county. At one such facility, dubbed Camp Selma, male inmates were crammed into a 50x18-foot cell and forced to stand on a wet concrete floor. They had no bedding or blankets. Women prisoners were treated similarly at a makeshift prison in Centreville.[8]

Most demonstrators, particularly working adults with children to care for and jobs to keep, were bailed out. But excessive bail was typically set for SCLC and SNCC staffers, and for students who had been arrested several times. Many remained jailed for days and some for weeks.

Whenever possible, black movement inmates were kept separate from the regular prisoners so as not to contaminate them with ideas such as speedy-trials, rights to an attorney, racially-unbiased justice, and other fanciful notions. But white civil rights workers were sometimes locked in with other white prisoners who were encouraged by the guards to show these "race traitors" the error of their ways.[9]

With the media engaged and white frustration mounting, the campaign again seemed to be back on track. And any doubts that King remained firmly in charge, even while jailed, are dismissed with a review of a to-do list he prepared in his cell and gave to Young, who was permitted several visits a day:

Do the following to keep national attention focused on Selma:

- Make a call to Governor Collins [of the Community Relations Service] and urge him to make a personal visit to Selma to talk with city and county authorities concerning speedier registration and more days for registering.

- Follow through on suggestion of having a congressional delegation to come in for personal investigation. They should also make an appearance at mass meeting if they come.
- Make personal call to President Johnson, urging him to intervene in some way.
- Urge lawyers to go to 5th circuit [court of appeals] if Judge Thomas does not issue an immediate injunction against continued arrests and speeding up registration
- Keep some activity alive every day this week.
- Consider a night march to the city jail protesting my arrest [an arrest which must be considered unjust]. Have another night march to courthouse to let Clark show [his] true colors.
- Stretch every point to get teachers to march.
- Immediately post bond for staff members essential for mobilization who are arrested.
- Seek to get big-name celebrities to come in for moral support.
- Get Wyatt [Walker] to contact Gov. Rockefeller and other Republican big names to come out with strong statements about the arrests, the right to vote and Selma.
- Call C. T. [Vivian] and have him return from California in case other staff is put out of circulation.
- Local Selma editor [Roswell Falkenberry of the Times Journal] sent telegram to [the] President calling for [a] congressional committee to come and study true situation of Selma. We should join in calling for this. By all means don't let them get the offensive. They are trying to give the impression that they are an orderly and good community because they integrated public

> accommodations. We just insist that voting is the issue and here Selma has dirty hands."[10]

King was still calling the shots, but his philosophy of nonviolent protest was about to be challenged by a national black leader with a sharply different message.

Chapter 6: A Visit from Malcolm X

On February 3, controversial black nationalist Malcolm X took an early-morning flight from New York City to Alabama. Landing in Montgomery at about noon, Malcolm then traveled the short distance to Tuskegee Institute, where he addressed an overflow crowd of students at Logan Hall. Even though 3,000 students managed to cram into the hall, hundreds more had to be turned away.[1]

Malcolm, like many in the movement, was undergoing a crisis of confidence. Having built a reputation as a virulent, anti-white racist through his association with the Nation of Islam, a radical black separatist group commonly referred to as the Black Muslims, Malcolm had been distancing himself from the Nation after breaking with leader Elijah Muhammad just over a year earlier.

Once the Nation's most prominent spokesman, Malcolm now found himself at odds with the organization's fundamental belief that all white people were devils and its ultimate goal of creating a self-sustaining black nation.

Notorious over the years for his pointed criticism of civil rights leaders and white politicians, Malcolm began to temper his message. He announced his opposition to all forms of bigotry and professed an eagerness to work with civil rights leaders and whites who genuinely supported black Americans.

Shortly after a spiritual trek to the holy city of Mecca, Saudia Arabia, Malcolm announced that he had converted to orthodox Sunni Islam and was establishing his own spiritual organization, Muslim Mosque, Inc.

Malcolm's presence in Alabama highlighted an interesting dynamic. His rhetoric, less strident than in the past but still provocative, coupled with the growing assertiveness of many young civil rights leaders, meant the once extreme Nation of Islam spokesman suddenly found himself closer to, if not actually in, the mainstream of rapidly evolving movement thought.

Inspired by Malcolm's message at Tuskegee, several students with ties to SNCC invited him to Selma, just 100 miles west. One day later, Malcolm addressed a hastily called mass meeting at Brown Chapel.

Malcolm's visit to Selma created an awkward situation. Although he had tempered his anti-white rhetoric since breaking with the Nation of Islam, Malcolm's racial philosophy was still far from King's vision of integration and harmony. And while his presence in Selma had been arranged by SNCC, the SCLC had signed on as a co-sponsor, with Andrew Young reasoning that "everyone has a right to be heard."[2]

In his presentation, Malcolm supported the intent of the Selma campaign, but not the SCLC's measured approach. "The black folks in this country ... have an absolute right to use whatever means necessary to gain the vote," he said. "I don't believe in nonviolence. The white man should thank God for [King and his followers] because they are giving white people time to get things in shape."

But Malcolm ended on a conciliatory note, saying:

"I'm not intending to try and stir you up and make you do something that you wouldn't have done anyway. I pray that God will bless you in everything that you do. I pray that you will grow intellectually, so that you can understand the problems of the world and where you fit into that world picture. And I pray that all the fear that has ever been in your heart will be taken out."

Following his speech, Malcolm sat down next to King's wife, Coretta, who was also scheduled to speak that night. According to Coretta King, Malcolm leaned over toward her and said, "Mrs. King, will you tell Dr. King that I'm sorry I won't get to see him. I want him to know that I didn't come to make his job more difficult. I thought that if the white people understood what the alternative was that they would be willing to listen to Dr. King."[3]

King later said he couldn't block Malcolm from visiting Selma, but that he himself never would have invited him. So different were their respective philosophies that King feared Malcolm's message would be disruptive and confusing to those in the midst of a nonviolent campaign.[4]

King's concerns were largely unfounded, but the fact that SNCC saw fit to reach out to Malcolm was itself a troubling sign, and another indication of growing differences between the two civil rights organizations.

Meanwhile, a concerted effort was being made behind the scenes to resolve the courthouse standoff. Selma's business leaders were growing increasingly unhappy with the negative publicity Clark's behavior was bringing to the city and urged local officials to strike a compromise that would result in the departure of the SCLC, the ubiquitous television cameras, and all those nosy reporters. The economic climate in Selma at the time was dismal, and business leaders feared that a protracted campaign would chase away investment dollars and prospective employers. They were searching for a way to back out of the national spotlight.

A SNCC report written at about this time took note of Selma's interest in attracting industry from the North, contending that televised images of racial discord were likely to derail any such initiatives. Of more immediate impact, the report observed, simply, that "white folks won't come to town and shop when demonstrations are going on."[5]

But even with many civic leaders seeking a truce, Selma's white underclass, getting its cues from Clark and Hare, was intent on foiling the black initiative, regardless of the tactics being used. If that meant some occasional violence, so be it. In that sense, the Selma dispute was not only white vs. black, or black vs. black, it had now also become white vs. white.

Also behind the scenes, Attorney General Nicholas Katzenbach was pushing hard for a peaceful resolution and devoted a considerable amount of time lobbying U.S. District Judge Daniel H. Thomas in Mobile for a restraining order that the black protesters might find acceptable.

Katzenbach had been acting attorney general since Robert Kennedy resigned in the fall of 1964 to run for the Senate from New York. Although concerned that Katzenbach was a "Kennedy man," President Johnson was impressed with his work on the 1964 Civil Rights Act and appointed him attorney general on January 31, 1965.

White moderates in Selma also urged Thomas to offer concessions, which, they hoped, would weaken the movement.

The aggressive lobbying campaign paid off on Thursday, February 4, when Judge Thomas issued a broad order prohibiting local officials from harassing potential registrants, eliminating use of the literacy tests, and demanding that registrars take at least 100 registrations on days they met. He also ordered the county to clear out its entire backlog of voter applicants by July 1.[6]

It was the first sign of a breakthrough. With the white establishment eager for the protesters to leave and at least some black residents growing weary of the struggle, the order seemed to be something with which both sides could live.

Young, who was nominally in charge while King was in jail, sounded a conciliatory note, suggesting that the SCLC might go elsewhere if local officials and the Dallas County Voters League found the agreement acceptable. Encouraged by Judge Thomas's order, Young and King's other SCLC lieutenants canceled demonstrations for Thursday afternoon.

But King was having none of it, and was dismayed that his top aides had been fooled by what he considered an obvious ploy designed to get Selma off the hook – and the front pages – in exchange for some empty promises that could easily be disavowed when the movement left town. From jail, King got an urgent message to Young, saying it was "a mistake" not to march. "Please don't be too soft," he said. "We have the offensive. In a crisis we must have a sense of drama. Don't let Baker control our movement. We may accept the restraining order as a partial victory, but we cannot stop."[7]

While others focused on the "concessions" in Thomas's order, King emphasized what the ruling *didn't* do. Thomas did not order that any blacks actually be added to the voter rolls, nor did he mandate any increase in the number of registration days. In addition, his ruling applied only to Dallas County and nowhere else in Alabama.[8]

King issued a press release emphatically stating that the pressure would increase and that the SCLC would be in Selma "for some time to come."[9]

Young got the message, telling the press in Selma, "Just as the 1964 Civil Rights bill was written in Birmingham, we hope that new federal voting legislation will be written here."[10]

Protests began again Friday morning, and some 500 marchers were arrested by Clark at the courthouse. Later that day, a discouraged Katzenbach told Johnson that the demonstrations had resumed despite the court order. "They've gotten about everything they wanted, but they're still demonstrating," he said. "I suppose they don't want to lose their momentum."

Johnson complained that the court order essentially gave King what he wanted. "This is what he asked for and this is what he got," the president said. "And we expect some quid pro quos."[11]

By that, Johnson meant he wanted King to be more willing to accept smaller victories in order to give the administration more time to prepare its voting rights bill. The president risked incurring significant political blowback from his embrace of civil rights. He was putting himself, and his party, on the line, and he didn't want King to take his support for granted.

Some media outlets also criticized King's perceived intransigence, with one prominent headline declaring "Negroes don't know what they want."

Early the next week, the movement faced a new "compromise" dilemma. Following King's instructions to keep the pressure on, Bevel rejected another idea pitched by Dallas County officials. Again hoping to stop the drumbeat of courthouse marches, county officials offered to provide a daily "appearance book" that potential voters could sign, reserving one of the hundred slots available for the next date on which the registrars would take applications.

Some movement leaders and their supporters viewed the offer favorably, but Bevel saw it as just one more attempt to divide movement participants. And by design or not, it worked. Bevel's decision to ignore the gesture angered members of the county Voters League. President Fred Reese thought the proposal offered real hope for Selma citizens to register, unlike the marches, which had accomplished little in nearly a month.

Reese's priority was to win Selma's black residents the vote so they could participate in the vital local decisions that affected their daily lives. "This is our movement," he reminded King. "You are our guests."

Reese added: "We should, at this point, shape a victory."[12]

Many other marchers also thought the battle had been won. But King and his advisors knew better. Though it sounded promising, the plan contained no guarantees and no real legal protection. Judge Thomas could not be present in the courthouse every day to monitor the procedures, meaning that the local registrars – the same registrars who had mastered the art of deception and delay – would be in charge. There were plenty of tricks to keep blacks from registering, and the Dallas County courthouse crowd knew them all.

Also, the local enforcer of the election laws would be the chief police officer of the county, Sheriff Jim Clark. For obvious reasons, that wouldn't do.

But there was more. For King, the goal was universal. The SCLC campaign was aimed at challenging the entire structure of voter disenfranchisement in the Deep South and to force President Johnson's hand on a federal voting statute.

Registering a couple hundred black voters in Alabama would not advance the cause.

King, therefore, was not about to accept any locally driven compromises that threatened the bigger picture. As usual, he managed to hold the campaign together and foster a sense of unity even when powerful internal forces were pulling him in different directions.

Though examined in detail and debated at length, King's prophet-like ability to inspire his followers and marshal support for his cause continues to confound historians. Part of his success certainly stemmed from his charismatic personality and dynamic oratorical skills, but other factors must be considered as well, most notably his ability to listen and analyze.

King made it a practice to say very little as his advisors debated a never-ending log of potentially divisive issues, contenting himself instead to listen to the lengthy, frequently heated discussions as a silent observer. However, when action was required, King would crisply summarize the issue and the various points of view, announce his decision, and then explain the rationale for that decision. As a result, even those whose perspectives had been rebuffed left feeling that at least their voices had been heard.

Some observers suggest that all of the above, coupled with his deeply religious background, allowed King to cast the movement as a spiritual crusade unbeholden to common earthly bonds. Others say King emerged in the right place at the right time, offering leadership and hope to a black America that was becoming increasingly urbanized, and thus more geographically concentrated. That, coupled with the rapid growth and popularity of television news, made it easier for King to spread his message.

But whatever inter-personal skills or sociohistorical changes might have been at work, credit must also go to King's innate sense of propriety and dogged determination to do what was morally right, at least as it pertained to movement strategy. This was, after all, a crusade for justice, equality and freedom, and King, recognizing the power of that platform, rarely if ever diluted it or allowed himself to be distracted by political concerns or personal differences. He was flexible on tactical issues and willing to compromise when the greater good was at stake, but never yielded on matters of principle.

Back on the streets of Selma, meanwhile, King's badge-bedecked nemesis was ever-present but for the most part resisted doing anything that would further inflame matters. Still, Sheriff Clark's appearance and mannerisms suggested nothing so much as a ticking time bomb. Hopeful campaign leaders were betting that it was just a matter of time before Clark would blunder again, and they were right.

Unable to stand his newfound prosperity, the sheriff stumbled badly when confronted by a contingent of underage marchers who were bolstering the ranks while the adults went to work.

On Wednesday, February 10, some 160 students marched to the courthouse carrying hand-lettered signs reading "Let Our Parents Vote," "Wallace Must Go," and "Jim Clark is a Cracker." By now, the courthouse protests had become routine, and everyone knew what to expect, but this time, Clark surprised them.

As Clark yelled, "Move out," his deputies and possemen herded the students down Alabama Avenue toward the jail, jabbing and poking them with their clubs. The students assumed they were being arrested, but instead of taking them to jail, the cops forced them to start running. Clark rode along in his car as the young protesters were forced down Water Street and then out on isolated River Road bordering the Alabama River swamps and sloughs.

One deputy reportedly yelled, "March, damn it, march! You want to march so bad, now you can march. Let's go!"

At the creek bridge, deputies used their cars to block the road so that reporters and photographers back at the courthouse, who were taken by surprise at Clark's change in tactics, couldn't catch up. Later, several students told reporters they were struck with clubs and jolted with cattle prods when they slowed their pace or attempted to rest. Some fled or were driven into the bogs and swamps while others managed to escape to a black-owned farm. Several youngsters returned with lumps on their heads and cuts on their faces. A nine-year-old boy who made the march with bare feet stood silently crying.[13]

Clark told reporters with a smirk that the student prisoners had escaped his custody, and John Lewis released a hastily prepared statement decrying the "inhuman, animal-like treatment of the Negro people of Selma."

But Clark had once again made a serious error in judgment. In fact, it was the same mistake made by Bull Connor, who had roughly mishandled young marchers in Birmingham a year earlier. Clark is often compared to Connor and the two were, in fact, ideological twins on the issue of race and law enforcement. However, Clark was the more visibly frightening of the two due to his military bearing and array of personal weaponry. Connor, who was 67 years old during the battles of Birmingham a year earlier, hardly seemed to merit his nickname. He was an unimposing figure with thinning white hair and an ever-present pair of wire-rimmed glasses. Born Theophilus Eugene Connor, his nickname likely derived from his hard-charging political style, not his personal appearance or physical strength.

Clark was as emotionally explosive as Connor, and he looked the part. All he lacked was a memorable nickname.

Reports of Clark's treatment of the youngsters generated a public opinion backlash against the sheriff that included some of his staunchest supporters. The Selma daily newspaper criticized him editorially, and white Selma businessmen called for restraint. Even the typically supportive White Citizens' Council, heretofore effusive in its praise of Clark, seemed to sense that things were spinning out of control. Hounded from all sides, Clark checked into a hospital for treatment of exhaustion.

This could have been construed as good news by the movement. The notorious sheriff was on the defensive and people who had thus far supported his tactics were now rethinking their position. But in the trenches of racial politics, things aren't always as they seem. With Clark temporarily sidelined, the voting rights campaign again lost momentum. Much of the reporting made it clear that white Selma did not universally support Clark, and, equally damaging, television footage revealed that many of those lining up to register at the courthouse were not of legal voting age. Also, due to Baker's influence, the chance of a photographer getting an inflammatory photograph anywhere but the courthouse was slim.[14]

Not surprisingly, Clark took a dim view of what he considered phony antics on the part of the protesters, contending that the entire setup was designed to generate controversy. He said the registration lines were full of non-residents and children below the age of 18 who would not have been able to register regardless of their race. "That was for the benefit of the cameras," he said. "It was just a complete farce as far as the whole act, and the press ... went right along with it."[15]

It was now apparent that the power of television cut both ways, and at least some of the support marchers had accrued earlier in the year dissipated when viewers sensed they were being manipulated by the movement's efforts to influence national television coverage for maximum effect. It was a delicate public relations dance for the protesters, who had to orchestrate news coverage with strong visuals without appearing manipulative, just as they had to elicit violent reactions to their efforts without appearing provocative.

Mayor Smitherman said the movement's reliance on televised drama was evident from the beginning and insisted that the SCLC didn't stumble into Selma by happenstance. "They picked Selma just like a movie producer would pick a set," he said later. "You had the right ingredients. I mean, you would have had to see Clark in his day. He had a helmet like General Patton and he had the clothes, the Eisenhower jacket and the swagger stick."[16]

Clark, in effect, was playing a leading role in a reality TV program produced by the SCLC long before there were reality TV programs, a fact he never seemed to grasp.

Meanwhile, many of the marchers had begun to tire and were eager to return to their daily routines. Black adults, whatever their racial philosophies, had livings to earn and could not spend their days standing in registration lines. Though to a person they remained committed to the cause, these adult marchers began scaling back their involvement to focus on other responsibilities, such as providing food for their families.[17]

Later in the day on February 10, King and his leadership council met to reassess the focus of the campaign. One of the major issues to be decided was whether to continue to concentrate on Selma, or devote more resources to the adjacent counties. King and Young argued for expanding the protests, fearing that the black people of Selma were tired and couldn't realistically be expected to maintain their rigorous protest schedule. The strategists agreed to push harder in surrounding Black Belt counties as a way to maintain momentum. That decision would have major ramifications for the campaign, most notably for the residents of Marion, but not until more unremarkable days had passed.

Often forgotten among the dramatic photographs and news footage of demonstration violence that erupted at so many marches across the South was the weary routine and chronic boredom with which the marchers had to contend. Day after day of marching, singing, and milling about seemingly without any tangible sense of accomplishment could dishearten even the most devoted demonstrator.

But march veterans knew that such inconveniences were a necessary means to the desired end. Without the pressure applied by the relentless presence of the marchers, municipal authorities would have no incentive to yield, nor would they have occasion to commit a public relations blunder. [18]

And so it went in Selma -- march and wait, march and wait.

Veteran movement journalists were beginning to wonder if Selma, apart from the courthouse, was raw enough to sustain the campaign. On February 14, in a *New York Times* news analysis, reporter John Herbers predicted that Selma was "not likely to become another Birmingham."

Indeed, the Selma campaign was beginning to wear on everyone involved. Locked into a grinding struggle, both sides were growing angry and frustrated. Tension was building and confrontations were becoming more personal. Movement veterans had been through it before and were girding themselves for an explosive outburst.[19]

Several days later, the Rev. C. T. Vivian, a feisty, no-nonsense member of the SCLC board, volunteered to take charge of the Selma demonstrations to see if he could breathe new life into them.

At 41, Vivian had earned the respect of his younger colleagues by taking an active role during the movement's early lunch counter sit-ins and the Freedom Rides of 1961, during which he and other SNCC protesters were arrested in Jackson, Mississippi and transferred to the notorious Parchman Prison Farm, where they were beaten and tortured. Later in 1961 King appointed Vivian as director of affiliates for the SCLC, making him responsible for coordinating the activities of branches nationwide.

Trusted by his SCLC colleagues and boasting a certain street cred with the younger, more aggressive SNCC operatives, Vivian was ideal for the role, and King quickly gave the move his blessing.

Vivian was determined to get the movement back on track. It didn't take long.

Chapter 7: Vivian vs. Clark

It was a cold, rainy mid-February morning when Vivian led his first march to the courthouse. Clark, out of the hospital and back on the job by now, maintained his watch of the marchers from inside the courthouse where he could avoid the chilly winds, but denied access to the demonstrators, who were forced to mill about outside.

That was unacceptable to Vivian. Bounding up the courthouse steps, he insisted on talking to Clark and then spared no words in denouncing him and demanding to be allowed to enter. Words were exchanged. Vivian claims he called Clark "an evil man." Clark says Vivian called him "Hitler, a brute and a Nazi."[1]

Regardless of who said what, Clark snapped. In full view of television cameras, he lunged at Vivian but was constrained by his deputies. In the melee that ensued, someone punched Vivian in the mouth, knocking him to the ground. Confusion still exists as to exactly who threw the punch. King aide Ralph Abernathy says it wasn't Clark himself, but most likely one of his deputies. However, televised footage, though inconclusive, seems to reveal that it was in fact Clark.

For his part, Clark acknowledged losing his temper but said he didn't recall throwing a punch. "The next thing I knew, he was at the bottom of the steps," Clark said. "I don't remember hitting him, but I went to the doctor and got an X-ray and found out I had a linear fracture in a finger on my left hand."[2]

"One of the first things I ever learned," Clark later bragged, "was not to hit a nigger with your fist because his head is too hard."

Once again the campaign had approached the thin line separating innocent nonviolent witness from deliberate provocation, but no matter, the results were the same. Clark and his cronies looked like heartless thugs, and Vivian, though physically injured, was the beneficiary.

Clark claims Vivian goaded him into acting. Vivian acknowledges forcing the issue with Clark but insists it was a matter of principle, not a ploy to provoke a violent response. "We had a right to be there. We had a right to vote, and here was the evil force that was stopping that," he said years later. "You do not walk away from that. You continue to answer it."[3]

Interviewed for the PBS *Eyes on the Prize* television documentary, Vivian said the fact that he was injured was irrelevant. "The only important thing is that you reach the conscience of those who are with you and of anyone watching — both the so-called enemy, and those who are preparing the battle, and anyone else who may be watching," he said.

"It was a clear engagement between those who wished the fullness of their personalities to be met, and those that would destroy us physically and psychologically," Vivian added. "This is what movement meant. Movement meant that finally we were encountering, on a mass scale, the evil that had been destroying us on a mass scale."

To back down, Vivian said, would have been to allow evil to destroy the forces of righteousness. "I had to get back up because otherwise people would have been defeated by violence," he said.[4]

And once again, Clark was the foil. As one SCLC leader remarked, casually, "Whenever things are looking bad, Sheriff Clark steps in to rescue us."

But while the civil rights community was inwardly celebrating the Clark-Vivian encounter and ensuing publicity, white Selma was seething at the movement's provocative tactics, contending, not without merit, that the activists were deliberately goading Clark and his colleagues into unseemly acts of violence.

The *Selma Times-Journal,* which seemed to be having trouble finding a consistent editorial voice on the demonstrations, lashed out at Vivian and the other "outside agitators" in a rare Page 1 editorial. One week after criticizing Clark for his forced march of student demonstrators, the paper was back on the side of the segregationists, calling for the "immediate departure of all outside forces, which now are deliberately provoking the understanding and sympathy of all sound-thinking citizens perilously near to the breaking point."

The editorial appeared to endorse black voting rights, but only to those not familiar with southern code: "No reasonable Dallas Countian denies that every citizen, regardless of race, is entitled to enfranchisement, *if he can legally qualify for it* (emphasis added). But while voting is a privilege of free people, it embodies solemn responsibility, *which should be entrusted only to competent citizens* (emphasis added)."[5]

Incredibly, the paper then applauded its white readers for their tolerance in the face of black effrontery. Such patience, it solemnly intoned, "is no menial accomplishment of self-control, and it is one which should command the respect of every well-meaning Selma Negro.

"This restraint," the editorial continued, "we regard as the ultimate expression of good faith by our white citizens."

Since the paper did not devote any space to an opposing point of view, there is no record of how the demonstrators -- the descendants of slaves and a century's worth of vile Jim Crow laws -- reacted to the "patience" and "good faith" of those who still refused to recognize them as equals.

The *Times-Journal*'s torturous rationalization aside, Clark had once again given demonstrators the upper hand. Black leaders celebrated their good fortune, while Smitherman, Baker and others bemoaned the sheriff's inability to control his temper.

First lampooned as a caricature of the redneck southern sheriff, Clark by now had become a caricature of himself. So soundly was he vilified, in fact, that one might almost be tempted to feel sorry for him. Could anyone really be as stubborn as the blustering sheriff? Could anyone really be so self-destructive?

In a word, yes.

Clark truly believed the protesters were seeking "black supremacy" and thus considered his actions not only appropriate but necessary. A year before his death in 2006 at age 84, Clark told the *Montgomery Advertiser*, "Basically, I'd do the same thing today if I had it to do all over again."[6]

Clark's 1966 book, *I Saw Selma Raped: The Jim Clark Story* is essential reading for anyone interested in a personal, unvarnished portrait of the sheriff. Defiantly determined to tell his side of the story, Clark manages only to confirm his reputation as a mean-spirited bigot. The slim, pamphlet-sized book reads more like a racist manifesto than a personal account of the previous year's events. With its outrageous conspiracy theories, total lack of regard for anyone not just like him and consistently defiant tone, Clark's book does nothing so much as reveal the inner workings of a white supremacist mind.

Clark describes those who arrived from out of state to join the demonstrations as "filthy, promiscuous degenerates," some of whom he suspected of being homosexuals or as he puts it "limp-wristed." One Selma resident, Clark reports, even saw a black man with his arm around a white man's shoulder.

The sheriff rails against "outside agitators" seeking to impose their will on the good (read: white) people of Alabama and insists change wasn't necessary because most of the area's black residents were content with their lot in life. They were being misled, he says, by the "bearded and the beatniks," the "blue-jeaned babes," the "rabble and the riff-raff."[7]

Clark reaffirmed that belief years later, telling an interviewer that race relations in Selma were very good until SNCC came to town in 1963. "They had lived there peaceably for 100 to 150 years between, the blacks and whites did, and there was no discontent on the part of either one as far as we could tell."[8]

It's quite likely that Clark really believed what he was saying. So thorough was the divide between the races during that era that whites would frequently congratulate themselves for taking good care of "our Negroes" and then express genuine surprise upon discovering that those same black folks wanted *more.*

Clark's response was emblematic of the feelings of betrayal being experienced by many white Selma residents who couldn't believe that their blacks, those same blacks who worked so hard and never uttered a discouraging word, would protest of their own volition. It has to be the work of those pesky outsiders, they mused. Without them our Negroes would still be happy.

Indeed, it was inconceivable to many of these people that the black residents they knew could be disenchanted with their lot in life, that they would actually aspire to anything more than the subservient roles for which they were so obviously intended. These whites had been listening to their black employees and neighbors tell them what they wanted to hear for so long that they actually began to believe they were content. For many, it was a shock to learn otherwise.

It was a situation similar to the surprise of white slave owners when they discovered during the Civil War that their servants were not perfectly satisfied with the lives they led. At that time, most slaves publicly supported their owners and the southern rebellion, but privately followed the course of the war through elaborate information grapevines, fervently hoping for a Union victory. A Tennessee slave named Isaac Lane said, "The best thing to do was to be friendly and loyal and obedient to massas til freedom come."[9]

But not all slaves harbored thoughts of freedom. Some were so downtrodden, they assumed their situation was unchangeable. "We didn't know nothing else but slavery, never thought of nothing else," said a man named Chapman, also of Tennessee. "I just know I belonged to the man who provided for me, and I had to take whatever he give me."[10]

Years later, Selma Mayor Smitherman struggled to put the black/white dynamic in context:

"I guess this just sounds silly today, but you just felt blacks were satisfied with the type life style they had, and I know it's very demeaning to say that, but you thought they were just satisfied living in these shacks and they were happy people. I mean you just grew up with that sort of thing cause you grew up with a lot of poverty yourself."[11]

******

On February 21, 1965, slightly more than two weeks after he visited Selma, activist Malcolm X was murdered while preparing to deliver a speech to a black unity group in Manhattan. Malcolm, who had invoked the wrath of Elijah Muhammad after leaving the Nation of Islam a year earlier, was gunned down by three men, all members of that Muslim group.

An estimated 15,000-30,000 mourners attended a public viewing over three days at a Harlem funeral home. The funeral itself was held February 27 at the Faith Temple Church of God in Christ in Harlem. The church was filled to capacity with more than 1,000 people. Loudspeakers were set up outside the temple so the overflowing crowd could listen and a local television station broadcast the funeral live. [12]

Among the civil rights leaders attending were Andrew Young, John Lewis, and James Forman. King sent a telegram to Malcolm's wife, Betty Shabazz, expressing his sadness over "the shocking and tragic assassination of your husband."

King said:

> *"While we did not always see eye to eye on methods to solve the race problem, I always had a deep affection for Malcolm and felt that he had a great ability to put his finger on the existence and root of the problem. He was an eloquent spokesman for his point of view and no one can honestly doubt that Malcolm had a great concern for the problems that we face as a race."* [13]

King's sadness was genuine. He knew that Malcolm spoke for many black people and considered him a potentially great leader, albeit one who had plenty of room to mature in judgment and statesmanship. In fact, King hoped that Malcolm's increasingly visible differences with Muhammad would prompt him to further temper his incendiary "hate whitey" rhetoric and nudge him in the direction of nonviolence. "It is unfortunate that this great tragedy occurred when Malcolm X was re-evaluating his own philosophical presuppositions and moving toward a great understanding of the nonviolent movement and toward more tolerance of white people," he told reporters.[14]

Although their methods and specific goals differed significantly, King and Malcolm X were both pursuing the same dream of black liberation.

The incident also forced King to ponder his own fragile sense of well-being. He was accustomed to receiving death threats, but the volume had increased in recent months, as had the savage nature of the threats. But if King was worried, he never let it show. Asked by newsmen if Malcolm's death had made him fearful for his own life, King responded with typical restraint: "I get threats quite often. This is almost a daily and weekly occurrence. I have learned now to take them rather philosophically ... One has to conquer the fear of death if he is going to do anything constructive in life and take a stand against evil."[15]

Chapter 8: The foot soldiers

"These humble children of God were willing to suffer for righteousness' sake."

Martin Luther King on the many unsung heroes of the civil rights movement

They are called "foot soldiers" and they are an indispensable part of any political campaign or social movement. They are young and old, male and female, black and white. What they might lack in organizational prowess or political experience, they more than recover in energy, determination and a fervent belief in their cause.

Movement leaders reap the headlines and prestigious awards, but foot soldiers are the people who actually make things happen, often at great personal sacrifice and the threat of bodily harm.

Most often, they are otherwise ordinary people -- teachers, farmers, laborers, small-business owners -- predisposed to worry more about providing for their families than changing the world, but when the cause is just and the time is right, they will do what has to be done, for the sake of their children if not themselves.

Conventional wisdom aside, the civil rights movement consisted of much more than a few larger-than-life figures, such as Martin Luther King. It was a movement built upon the determination and selflessness of countless individuals, all of whom found some way to contribute to the cause.

Foot soldiers kept the voting rights movement alive in Alabama during the cold days of January and February, 1965, by virtue of their willingness to endure long hours in line at the registrar's office, transport their neighbors to mass meetings and encourage colleagues whose spirits were flagging. Most sacrificed time with their families and many lost their jobs as a result of this singular commitment. All knew of the physical dangers they were courting. Still, the foot soldiers of Alabama refused to be deterred, giving campaign leaders the broad, unflinching support they required.

Most communities were blessed to have such committed movement supporters, but none were more devoted to the cause than the black residents of Marion, a tiny town tucked away in Perry County, a rural, forested county dotted with cattle ranches and dairy farms, some 30 miles northwest of Selma.

If Selma is the town that time forgot, Marion is the town time never knew. A much smaller version of Selma, Marion is a mostly black, impoverished community that offers its residents only the most basic amenities – a gas station or two, a bank, a post office, a supermarket and a few clothing stores. Lottie's Restaurant sits across the street from a one-room library. A seedy Chinese restaurant is just up the street, and fast-food franchises are conspicuous by their absence. A new motel sits on the outskirts of town, but its parking lot is vacant.

Like many such communities, Marion is dominated by a park-like town square, the middle of which is occupied by the Perry County Courthouse. Though not nearly as visible as other civil rights landmarks – the Selma bridge, Birmingham's 16th Street Baptist Church, Central High School in Little Rock, Arkansas -- that square was the setting for one of the most significant, and violent, events of the civil rights era.

******

Preston Hornbuckle has lived in Marion, Alabama, his entire life. Hornbuckle was born in 1934, the oldest of 10 children, and spent his early years attending school and working with his father, a local sharecropper. He held a number of jobs over the years before semi-retiring to his small farm on the outskirts of town.

Today, he and his wife, Dorothy, farm their land – turnips, collard greens, sweet potatoes, peas, corn, watermelon and

what he calls "rattlesnake beans," – keeping some of what they grow for themselves and selling the rest at the Marion farmer's market. "I got a heap of spare time now," he laughs, but it's unclear if he's joking.

Fit and spry, yet physically unimposing, Hornbuckle combs his black/gray hair straight back and displays the wisp of a gray moustache. Unprompted, he shares that his grandmother's father – his great-grandfather – was a white man. "That was pretty common back then," he says of sexual relations between black women and their white overseers.

Hornbuckle speaks quietly and deliberately, commanding the attention, and respect, of his listeners. Despite having an education that went no further than ninth grade, his understanding of the human condition, expressed in a disarmingly folksy manner, is profound. He has a hearty laugh and a surprisingly sly sense of humor.

Hornbuckle was involved from the beginning of the Marion civil rights movement. "I was in it all the way," he says. "I figured it was important because a whole lot of things that was goin' on weren't right. You couldn't vote, didn't matter how much education you had. My wife, she couldn't vote and she was a registered nurse."

In the mid-1960s, Hornbuckle and the other Marion foot soldiers were fighting the same race-based inequities that had bedeviled their predecessors for more than 100 years. Whites had settled Perry County in the early 19th Century, and black slavery quickly followed. Through the decades, the white power structure easily kept Perry County's black residents poor, segregated, and subject to countless indignities. As in nearby Selma, the result was a mostly demoralized black community, resigned to its plight and unwilling to discuss issues of race and segregation for fear of retaliation.[1]

Marion was described by attorney J. L. Chestnut as one of "Alabama's citadels of racism." But while many of Marion's black citizens might have been discouraged by their hostile environment, they also were also proud and self-reliant. Andrew Young found in Marion, "hard-working blacks who represented a ... pure, unpretentious solid folk force I could learn from and work with."[2]

All these people needed was someone to help them realize their situation wasn't hopeless and their circumstances didn't have to be permanent. That someone turned out to be Albert Turner, co-founder and first president of the Perry County Civic League.

Turner, then in his late 20s, was descended from slaves who had picked cotton locally. He grew up in a four-room shack just outside of Marion. Turner was a rarity – one of the few Alabama-born black men who went to college and graduated during the early 1960s. Upon returning to Marion, he tried to register to vote but failed the test, which was administered by a white man with a fifth-grade education.

Devastated by the hypocrisy and unfair treatment, Turner devoted much of his life's work to the civil rights movement and became legendary in Marion for his efforts to secure the right to vote. He spoke at churches and civic clubs and even went house to house in search of interested black residents.[3]

Chestnut, a longtime friend, said of him, "Whenever there was something of unusual danger, and nobody wanted to, you could count on the fact that Albert . . . would lead it."[4]

Turner's efforts attracted the attention of Willie Nell Avery, who had moved to Marion from neighboring Dallas County with her husband James in early 1962. Both became active in the Civic League.

In her early 20s at the time, Avery recognized that the right to vote held the key to genuine black independence and was determined to do everything she could to help secure that right. The first step was registering to vote herself.

She tried. Then she tried again. And again.

For 18 months, beginning in February 1962, Avery, a public school teacher with a college degree, was unable to register to vote in Perry County. She took the so-called literacy tests, but was never told how she did. "They wouldn't approve me or deny me," she recalled 50 years later. "They would just say, 'We haven't graded you yet.'"

Every two weeks, Avery would visit the courthouse to check on her status, and every time the answer was the same: "Not yet." The atmosphere was chilly, almost hostile. "They wouldn't even look up at me," she says. "They weren't friendly at all." On one visit, she noticed that her voter application form was marked "CW" in pencil. Willie Nell's heart sank. Having thus been flagged as a "colored woman," she knew her application was unlikely to be approved anytime soon.

Hornbuckle also cited the county's literacy tests as the single biggest obstacle to black voter registration. "I tried and tried but couldn't never pass that test," he says. "It was just a strange bunch of made-up questions. You'd need a Philadephia lawyer to get the answer to some of those questions."

Drawing an apt rural Alabama analogy to illustrate the futility of the literacy tests, Hornbuckle says, "It was like if you going on a raccoon hunt, they want to know how many raccoons you gonna catch before you go." It wasn't funny at the time, of course, but he can now laugh at the absurdity of it all. Still, the hurt remains.

"That was a terrible time," he says. "You got to ask God for the strength to carry you through."

Hornbuckle, Avery and other Marion foot soldiers – those that remain -- are aging now, but few have trouble recalling the hardships and indignities that sparked their activism some 50 years ago.

"We just didn't have any rights at all," says John Ward, a good-natured man with a head of thinning, snow-white hair. "Everything belonged to the whites."

Ward and his wife, Annie, tell by-now familiar segregation-era stories of separate drinking fountains, separate restrooms and race-specific restaurants. Everything designated "Colored" was inferior to its white counterpart, whether by age, size, cleanliness, or accessibility.

"Even at the bus station," says Mattie Atkins. "We had to wait in a little hole and they (whites) had a big room."

One of their biggest grievances involved the designation of separate treatment rooms and patient priorities at area doctor offices. Whites would have one room and blacks another, and blacks typically would not be seen until all the white patients had been treated.

"Whites would come in after we had arrived and get treated first," says Avery. "We would be the last to get waited on by the doctor."

This was more than just another slight to be endured; it was literally a matter of life and death. Hornbuckle lost his father to this particularly cruel Jim Crow practice:

"Back then, things were really tough for black people. We didn't have a chance. And what little chance we had, they tried to take it. They didn't want us to get no power. Now, my daddy, we carried him to the doctor's office. White people would come in and go right on in. But my daddy was sick, sick, sick. He later died on that doctor's office floor. And they never did get to wait on him. They could've done somethin' for him but they didn't do nothin'. My daddy was 84. He was an old man. But you know, age ain't got nothin' to do with how you bein' treated. I ain't holdin' that against nobody, but that's still inside me."

Even seemingly minor incidents contributed to the toxic racial environment of mid-60s Marion. Hornbuckle tells the story of a young female cousin who was picking cotton for a penny a pound and was determined to earn a dollar:

"My cousin, she picked 99 pounds and the man gave her 99 cents. She cried. She wanted that dollar so badly. She said, 'You could give me a dollar.' But he wouldn't give her a dollar. He gave her exactly 99 cents. I won't forget that if I live 'til 100."

Like blacks across the entire South, Marion residents silently coped with the pain because they didn't seem to have any viable alternatives.

"That's what we was used to," Atkins says softly.

"We were tough," John Ward adds. "We were survivors."

But one day, Annie Ward says, the long-suffering black population cried "Enough!"

"We decided to get up and unite, and do something about it," she says. "That's when the 60s came in and we thought we should have our rights, too."

Avery picks up the tale: "We thought about the Bible and how they marched along the walls of Jericho and the walls came tumbling down. We decided we would do that, too. So we started marching, and that upset them so badly. And we weren't saying anything. They were peaceful marches."

In late January 1965, the SCLC intensified its efforts in Marion and other Black Belt communities surrounding Selma. James Bevel's original plan had called for demonstrations in several towns simultaneously, and while the press focused on Selma, organizational efforts had been going on across the region.[5]

Marion was the most active of the outlying campaigns due in large part to Albert Turner's excellent work, as well as its core group of dedicated foot soldiers.

Legal efforts aimed at eliminating voter discrimination had been under way in Alabama for years. But an overwhelmed U.S. Department of Justice was no match for the delay tactics and clever tricks of southern officials determined to keep blacks out of the voting booth.

Willie Nell Avery's husband, James, was summoned to Mobile in early 1963 for a federal court hearing on voting rights. The Justice Department had filed suit against Perry County for alleged voter discrimination, and Judge Daniel Thomas was taking testimony.

Willie Nell attended the hearing and was furious with what she heard. James was a college graduate who had been

deemed unfit to vote, yet several white residents of Perry County admitted that they registered despite being unable to read or write. Avery discovered that whites were frequently permitted to take the literacy test home with them to get help with the answers.

The feds actually won a preliminary injunction prohibiting voter discrimination, but the practical effect was negligible. As expected, the Perry County Board of Registrars continued to discriminate against black voters in a variety of imaginative ways, all the while pretending to be acting in good faith.

Shortly after returning to Marion, both Willie Nell and James were told that their registrations had been approved. At the time, it was very unusual for both a husband and wife to be registered, but Willie Nell wasn't surprised. "They knew I had gone to Mobile and they knew my husband had testified in Mobile," she says. "They thought if they approved the two of us we would stop [campaigning for the right to vote.]"

The county officials who approved the Averys on that premise either didn't know them very well or were poor judges of character. Willie Nell and James redoubled their efforts on behalf of their less fortunate black neighbors, marching and protesting in support of others seeking the right to vote.

The registration poll tax at that time was $1.50, but Willie Nell refused to pay. "I told them, I'm not paying any tax for the right to vote," she says. "They gave me the card anyway."

******

One of the more promising components of the Civil Rights Act of 1960 was a provision for "federal referees," supposedly unbiased and objective observers who would rule on disputed registration decisions. On the surface, it looked like a good step forward, but critics predicted the referee provision would prove ineffective, and they were right.

By 1963, not a single referee had been appointed.

Nearly three years after the U.S. had filed its suit against Perry County, Judge Thomas finally appointed a referee, Ozmus Sigler Burke, a white lawyer from Hale County, where the black registration rate was even lower than that of Perry County. But Burke was no more interested than most of his colleagues in improving black access to the ballot box. Brian Landsberg, author of *Free at Last to Vote,* said that by appointing Burke, Thomas appeared to be taunting the Court of Appeals, saying, in effect, "You want a referee? I'll give you a referee!"[6]

Instead of ensuring fairness, Burke created additional headaches for prospective black voters, giving them even more forms to fill out and imposing additional obstacles to overcome. As one northern congressman had predicted in 1960, the plan froze into place the inequities that existed in the South by having a "southern judge, under all of the southern pressures, appoint a southern referee to pass judgment upon the problem that we have in the South."[7]

Even with a so-called "referee," southern pols were determined to subvert legal efforts to remedy the unfair registration process and had little trouble doing so. The problem was supposedly rectified in the Civil Rights Act of 1964, which clarified standards, added some teeth to the law and also forbade registrars from rejecting prospective voters for "insignificant" errors. As noted earlier, however, the law was no match for county and state officials intent on subverting it.

One of the applicants judged by referee Burke was Jimmie Lee Jackson, who had lived in Perry County since his birth in 1938. His answers to the test questions were legible and responsive, but in October 1964, Burke found Jackson – along with 110 other applicants – "not qualified under state law to vote." He gave no reason for his conclusions.

There was no way of knowing at that time, of course, but Jackson's confrontation with an Alabama state trooper just four months later would dramatically alter the course of the civil rights movement.

******

All of the ineffective and time-consuming legal maneuvering left the black residents of Marion and the rest of Perry County dispirited and disillusioned. When it came to marching, many of the town's adults weren't sure they wanted to get involved, considering it a futile exercise. Though most, if not all, believed in the cause, many also had practical concerns to weigh, most notably whether they wanted to put their jobs, or even their families, at risk.

So in late January 1965, Albert Turner, who by this time had been appointed Alabama field secretary for the SCLC and was one of King's top advisers, decided to supplement the ranks of his core foot soldiers. Swiping a page from James Bevel's Birmingham playbook, Turner called on the area's children to get involved.

The notion of using children for political purposes was controversial within the movement. Many civil rights leaders considered it exploitive and dangerous. But as the Birmingham campaign proved, it was also effective.

Bevel had been faced with a stalled campaign when he arrived in Birmingham in April, 1964. Over the objections of more senior SCLC leaders, he created a "children's crusade" comprised mostly of high school students. It worked better than anyone had hoped, and what was looking like a major defeat for King turned into a stunning victory.

Turner and his foot soldiers hoped to duplicate that success. "When we couldn't get the adults active, the children were encouraged to take part," Avery says simply. "They left school, marched and they were arrested."

February 1 was a tumultuous day in Marion. Following a march that resulted in the arrests of hundreds of adults, several hundred students – most of them singing freedom songs -- marched out of Morning Star Baptist Church to support voting rights for their parents. A state trooper with little appreciation for music reportedly told SCLC organizer James Orange, "Sing one more song and you're under arrest."

The singing continued and the students were arrested. But because the tiny county jail couldn't hold more than a handful of prisoners, the students were loaded onto Marion school buses and taken to a larger makeshift prison site where they were crammed into a bare concrete stockade and forced to drink from cattle-troughs.

The delicate situation was explained to worried parents at a mass meeting that night, and while the ploy might have upset some, it inspired others to get involved. Many more adults showed up the next day for a march around the courthouse.

Mattie Atkins was one of the newcomers. She was inspired by her niece, who had marched with some other school kids a day earlier. When she visited the Atkins home that afternoon, the niece gave Mattie a big hug and then, addressing Mattie's husband, proudly announced, "Guess what, Uncle Ison, I marched yesterday." Startled, Ison Atkins responded, "Marched! What for?" His niece said, "So we can get the right to vote."

Insert photo of Mattie Atkins She continued, excitedly, "We went into all the places that said 'Whites only,' and we drank out of the water fountain and we went to the bathroom. Everywhere it says 'Whites only, that's where we went. And guess what. We goin' back tomorrow."

Ison warned the youngster that she risked being arrested if she returned the next day, but that didn't stop her. The niece and many of her young friends marched despite the threat of arrest, earning themselves a trip to the county jail.

"Sure enough," Mattie says. "They loaded all of 'em up – three busloads – and put 'em in prison."

The authorities kept the children in custody overnight, telling relatives they would just have to wait. As the Atkinses waited, they thought about their niece's courage and the important issues at stake. They decided that they too would get involved.

"That's how we started marching," Atkins says. "My husband, myself, and my father-in-law. That was January, and it was cold. And we never stopped marching."

Willie Nell Avery, who was leading the February 1 march, was flanked by two young, white demonstrators from northern Alabama who were instructed to protect her should violence erupt.

As the group was completing another verse of "Ain't Gonna Turn Me Around," a state trooper stepped in front of Avery and put his billy club across her chest, halting the march.

"They didn't hit me," she says, "but they pulled those two white boys out of line and beat them mercilessly. There was blood flowing everywhere."

With all the attention focused on King's Selma campaign, demonstrations in Marion and other remote parts of the state received little if any widespread public notice, partly because they lacked "star power" and partly because news organizations had to determine where best to concentrate their limited resources.

The Marion foot soldiers were disappointed but not discouraged by the lack of attention . They did what they could for the movement, convinced that their efforts would eventually make a difference.

Today, Avery, Hornbuckle, Ward and many others are proud of what their activities helped to achieve but tend not to dwell on the past, preferring instead to live for the moment in the company of their children and their children's children

Chapter 9: Marion explodes

Thursday, February 18 dawned cool and clear in Marion, where civil rights demonstrators had been marching in relative obscurity virtually every day for the better part of a month. As in nearby Selma, the mood was tense, and most veteran observers feared it was just a matter of time before a spark of some sort resulted in serious, perhaps deadly, violence.

The afternoon edition of the *Selma Times-Journal,* with its patronizing editorial about the limits of white patience and the need for "thinking blacks" to step forward, was already on the streets as the Marion marchers began preparing for their next event, a march to be held that night.

Organizers knew night marches were especially dangerous but were determined to proceed. They had marched earlier that day, but wanted to intensify their efforts – "up the tempo," as Albert Turner said – so a decision was made to go both day and night.

The Thursday night march was in support of SCLC organizer Rev. James Orange, one of King's most loyal field staffers, who was in the Perry County jail. Orange had been arrested on a trumped up "disturbing the peace" charge commonly used to silence black protesters, and rumors were circulating that his jailers intended to kill him. Despite his imposing physique – Orange stood 6-3 and weighed more than 300 pounds – he was a strict disciple of the nonviolence philosophy and routinely endured beatings rather than retaliate. Andrew Young fondly referred to Orange as a "gentle giant."[1]

Meanwhile, Willie Nell Avery, who was working at a building near city hall that morning, noticed something odd. State troopers were driving up Highway 14 at regular intervals, each carrying several trooper uniforms for delivery to city hall. So as not to arouse suspicion, Avery said, the cars didn't come right after one another, but only after a decent amount of time had passed. "I stopped working and just watched," she said. "And when I went home I told my husband, 'there's something peculiar going on.' All these cars coming up the hill all day and when people weren't paying attention, then another one would come."

Avery wasn't sure what to make of this unusual development, but she was savvy enough to know it didn't bode well for that night's march.

Marion organizers had asked the SCLC to dispatch one of its Selma operatives to Marion to help call attention to the march, but with many of King's aides either out of town or otherwise indisposed, the choices were few. C. T. Vivian was eventually selected to drive over from Selma to speak at the meeting, but he wasn't happy about it. Vivian was bogged down in his Selma work and wasn't sure he could spare the time to go to Marion. "When they called me, I told them 'Look, now, I will come over and give the speech, but I've got to get right back to Selma. I can't lead the demonstration.' So I come on over and gave the speech."[2]

Arriving at Zion United Methodist Church for a mass meeting that would precede that night's march, Avery's worst fears were confirmed. Along with a small group of Marion policemen surrounding the grounds were about fifty Alabama state troopers and a ragged collection of local white thugs, all outfitted in state trooper uniforms. "The local people had been deputized," Avery said. "They put on all the uniforms I saw earlier that day."

Immediately after finishing his speech, Vivian was hustled out the back door and down the steps to an awaiting car. The scene was illuminated by a full moon that bathed everything in an eerie glow. Shadows darted, but the night seemed mostly still.

"When I got to a place where you turn, there was a state policeman standing there with a flashlight directing cars," Vivian recalled. "About a half dozen state cars had already passed us – zoom, zoom, zoom – and we figure, What's this all about?"[3]

The next 20 minutes or so would tell.

******

The demonstrators had a simple plan for that night. They would walk from the church, past the post office, the bus station, and a couple of small businesses to the jail, which was just one block away. There, they would sing movement songs to let Orange know they supported him. It would be short and, hopefully, uneventful.

As it turned out, very few marchers even made it to the post office.

The meeting having concluded, the 400 or so people inside the church were eager to begin marching, but they first had to be reminded of march protocol. As the demonstrators lined up to leave the church, Turner and other organizers called for silence and reminded them that under no circumstances were they to resort to violence. "If you can't commit to this, just stay inside," Turner said. "We don't want you marching."

"They didn't want us to be fighting back," said marcher Preston Hornbuckle. "They said, 'if you can't go out peacefully, stay in the church.'"

Meanwhile, Col. Al Lingo, commander of the Alabama State Troopers, took direct command of the troopers and pseudo-troopers, deploying them at 20-foot intervals along the sidewalk adjacent to the church. The troopers were in riot gear, helmets strapped in place, billy clubs held lengthwise at chest level.[4]

As planned, the men were the first to exit the church. Pushing the heavy double doors open at 9:25 p.m., they stepped outside into the cool night air and proceeded down the front steps of the church, frightened but determined. But before they could get more than a few steps up the street, they were stopped by Marion Police Chief T. O. Harris, who ordered them to halt.

"This is an unlawful assembly," Harris said. "You are hereby ordered to disperse. Go home or go back in the church."

Rev. James Dobynes, who was leading the march along with Turner and Rev. R. T. Johnson, called out, "May we pray before we go back?" Not waiting for an answer, Dobyne knelt and began, "Dear Lord God ..." At that moment, the streetlights went out, cloaking the entire scene in darkness. A police officer stepped forward and whacked Dobynes across the head with his nightstick. The kneeling Dobynes was an easy target for several other nearby cops, who started beating him under cover of night.

"That was probably the viciousest thing I had ever seen," Turner said. "They beat him and they took him by the heels and they drug him to jail."

Dobynes himself told the FBI the next day that the group had planned all along to return to the church if stopped, following his prayer. He confirmed that he was struck in the head as he knelt to pray. As he was being dragged toward the jail, he continued to pray and ask for help.

"One of the men [dragging me] kept telling me to get up and then he would bust me back down," Dobynes said. "They pushed me into jail and put me in a cell and one of the men kept saying "You ought to bleed to death, you black motherfucker." Dobynes was told the next day he had been charged with unlawful assembly. Bail was set at $50.

Perry County Sheriff W. U. Loftus told a different story. Loftus said Dobynes was not struck while he was in line. In fact, he told the FBI he didn't see anyone struck by any of the troopers, but claimed that someone threw a piece of concrete at the troopers as the marchers got near the bus station.[5]

As Loftus apparently was looking elsewhere, law enforcement officers and their ragtag posse, wildly swinging their billy clubs, began pushing the marchers back to the church entrance. Panic ensued when the marchers were unable to re-enter the church because the doorway was clogged by a throng of would-be marchers preparing to *exit* the church. Only 100 or so had been able to leave the church before violence erupted.

"After they started beating people outside, they tried to follow the men back into the church," Annie Ward recalled. "And Shorty Turner and Willie Lester Martin took some old wooden chairs and broke them and started fighting, and they wouldn't let them in. They were gonna come in and get us 'cause we couldn't run 'cause we were trapped."

The loss of lighting around the town square has long been a subject of debate. Some say the lights were shot out. Police blamed the marchers, saying only the outside church lights were turned off, and they were controlled by a switch from inside the church.

But those who were marching that night are certain that Marion authorities deliberately cut the power, plunging the entire city into darkness. "They planned to do it all along," John Ward said. "They wanted to make this city pitch dark."

Why? Ward has a theory. "They didn't want us to recognize the local people that were beating us," he said. "They could hit us without light." Ward then related the story of a black man on the ground about to be beaten who suddenly recognized his would-be assailant and called him by name. The man with the billy stick backed off.

The violence was arbitrary and unrestrained. Two marchers managed to straggle back into the church. Both had been clubbed over the head. "I wiped the blood off those two men that night," Annie Ward said. "Everyone was hollering and crying and no one knew what to do."

Rev. R.T. Johnson came in, raised his arms and told everyone to be peaceful. His hands were covered with blood.

John Ward was among those unable to get out of the church before the beatings began. He went to the windows to find out what was going on and was stunned by what he saw. "There were people running down along the side of the church," he said. "And there were women, you know, and they were just whipping them like everybody else. They were running alongside the church through the shrubbery, and it was just a mess."

Hornbuckle fled the police beatings by running to Mack's Café, just behind the church. "The cops was trying to push us back in the church by puttin' that stick on you," he said. "So a bunch of us went down to the café." Shortly after reaching the café, state troopers arrived and ordered everyone out. Hornbuckle explained what happened next:

> *"I had another feller with me, named David Herd, so I said, 'Let's go, David,' and when I went out, they popped me right side the head, almost staggered me. I made it to my car and got in, and then David came out. He seen them hit me, so he was on the lookout for it. So when they went to get him, they hit him on the shoulder. He said, 'I thought they just wanted us to come out. I didn't know they were gonna hit us,' Then he saw them hit me and he knew they were gonna try to hit him. We didn't want any trouble, we were just trying to get away from them."*

Hornbuckle returned home, where his wife cleaned and dressed the blood-soaked gash on his head. To this day, Hornbuckle carries a scar from the blow he received on the back of his head, but he didn't retaliate. "I didn't hit nobody back because they told us they didn't want no violence," he said.

And while he has forgiven the trooper that struck him, Hornbuckle says the incident is impossible to forget. "It always stays with you," he said.

Elijah Rollins, the owner of Rollins Funeral Home, was at a small club upstairs at Mack's when the violence erupted. Enjoying a beer with several friends, Rollins heard what he first thought was loud singing coming from below but quickly realized it was shouting and then screaming. Rushing to the window, Rollins saw troopers swinging their clubs at the people leaving Mack's.

Rollins didn't find out until the next day that one of those people had been shot by a state trooper. Eight days later, he was in charge of Jimmie Lee Jackson's funeral arrangements.

The bloody beatings weren't confined to the area around the church. The rampaging troopers and their newly deputized friends were lashing out against blacks who hadn't even been involved in the march, including those who worked out of town and were just arriving home, unaware of what was going on.

One young black man reportedly told a trooper he wasn't part of the march, to which the cop responded, "Well you should have been over there, because we're gonna knock your lights out anyway."

Louis Townes of Marion and two friends were parked near Zion United Methodist during the melee when troopers approached and ordered them to unlock the doors. They were then dragged from the car and shocked with cattle prods. Townes said troopers jolted him with the prods on his face and legs. One trooper then said, "Get on home."

Willie Nell Avery told the story of another man, J. C. Lewis, who was coming home from work when troopers stopped his car and beat him by the side of the road, nearly killing him. To avoid further beating, Lewis played dead, lying in a ditch and holding his breath until the troopers left. "They just left him laying there," Avery said. "He had to crawl home."

Lewis actually managed to walk to the home of Col. Paul Robinson, dean of students at the Marion Military Institute, where Lewis worked in the kitchen. Robinson answered the knock on his door at about 11:30 p.m. and found Lewis, who was bleeding from the top of his head. Lewis asked Robinson to help him get medical attention. Robinson dressed and took Lewis to the Perry County Hospital, where he was admitted.

According to FBI reports, Lewis told Robinson he was driving along Greensboro Highway out of Marion shortly after 11 p.m. when he was stopped by state police and asked for his driver's license. Robinson said Lewis told him he complied, but then was beaten for no apparent reason

As one witness told the FBI, you didn't have to be a marcher to get beaten that night, you just had to be black.

Even the most strident opponents of integration had a hard time defending police activities that night. The *Alabama Journal,* a segregationist newspaper, was appalled, calling the mayhem "a nightmare of State Police stupidity and brutality."

The Marion police/posse riot is one of the most underreported events of the Civil Rights era, with most books covering the story in just a paragraph or two. There are several reasons for that. As noted earlier, Marion is an isolated community, and with all of the movement's best-known figures focusing on Selma, the small town marches received minimal attention from the national press.

There were, in fact, a few reporters and television cameras in place at Marion, but the reporters were penned off and the cameras either confiscated or destroyed by police, so there are no still images or video footage of the riot. Then, of course, there is the fact that the event took place in the dark.

Reporters who tried to get closer to the action themselves were beaten. One, Richard Valeriani of NBC News, said a particularly nasty crowd had gathered that night. "We knew we were in trouble right away because people came up and started spraying the cameras with paint," he said. "Then they'd insist that we put the cameras down."[6]

Valeriani was struck from behind with a club, sending blood streaming down the back of his head. A white man who witnessed the incident walked up to a stunned Valeriani and asked, "Do you need a doctor?"

"Yeah, I think I do," Valeriani responded. "I'm bleeding."

The man leaned closer to him and snarled, "Well, we don't have doctors for people like you."[7]

Two UPI cameramen were beaten as troopers watched.

"I can still picture that night, the things that were going on," John Ward said. "It was awful."

At the peak of the violence, New York Times reporter John Herbers spotted Dallas County Sheriff Jim Clark wearing sports clothes and carrying a billy club. "'Don't you have enough trouble of your own over in Selma,' someone asked the sheriff," Herbers wrote. Clark replied: "Things got a little too quiet for me over in Selma tonight and it made me nervous."[8]

Chapter 10: Jimmie Lee Jackson is shot

By most accounts, Jimmie Lee Jackson was a nice young man, not the sort who would go looking for trouble. He was quiet, relatives say, always smiling, eager to please.

Unfortunately, much of Jackson's life is shrouded in mystery. With little or no public documentation available, the story of Jackson's life unfolds haphazardly in the maddeningly imprecise and conflicting accounts of his contemporaries, many of whom have long since passed, leaving an aging few to share their hazy recollections.

No one has anything negative to say about Jackson, but nor do they have much to provide beyond broad generalizations and folksy platitudes. The portrait they paint is of a pleasant enough young man, but it lacks the detail and depth needed for a more profound understanding.

All seem to agree that Jackson was a strong but gentle man. Born in December 1938 in Marion, he apparently worked at several different jobs during his short life, but the chronology and tenure are lost to history. At one time, he was employed as an orderly at a Perry County health facility. He also worked six days a week as a pulpwood cutter in the thick forests of west-central Alabama, his day typically extending from dawn until dusk. On Sundays, Jackson served as a deacon at his church.

Then there is the question of Jackson's military service, if any. One prominent observer, Andrew Young, contends in his autobiography that Jackson was a military veteran who served in Vietnam. Others say Jackson was indeed a veteran, but never served overseas. When his enlistment was up, they say, he returned home to help out at his grandfather's farm just outside of Marion. Still others contend that Jackson never served in the military.

But on one point at least, the friends and relatives are unanimous. All say that Jackson had a special regard for his elders. "Jimmie Lee loved helping out the older folks," said one distant relative, summarizing a sentiment shared by many others.

Jackson's affinity for the elderly was most apparent in his relationship with his 82-year-old grandfather, Cager Lee, a frail but energetic man with leathery brown skin and thin wisps of white hair.

Jimmie Lee would do anything for the old man, and Cager Lee in turn served as mentor, friend, and father-figure to his grandson. No one who knew them would deny that theirs was a special relationship.

Cager Lee relied on Jackson to help maintain the modest family farm, which also served as home to Jackson's younger sister, Emma Jean, and their mother, Lee's daughter, Viola.

Actually, referring to the family's farm as "modest" is being charitable. Like many other rural black residents, the Jacksons lived in a shack without running water or electricity. Furniture consisted of a small table and a few chairs. Outside, open sewage ran in a stream through the backyard.[1]

Lee also counted on Jackson to help him get around town, tend to various appointments and, most significantly, accompany him to civil rights movement activities, which had spread from Selma to Marion in early 1965.

Despite his advanced age, Cager Lee was active in the movement, but questions persist as to the extent of his grandson's involvement. Published reports routinely identify Jackson as a civil rights activist, which might be true. But it also might just be a tidy story line. And therein lies the source of one of the Selma/Marion movement's most contentious disputes.

Many of those who knew Jackson say he played an active role in the Marion protests. Others disagree, saying Jackson was content to remain on the sidelines, wary of committing too much time or energy, perhaps because of his many other responsibilities. But regardless of his actual level of involvement, Jackson supported the movement and had attempted at least once to register to vote.

Although his application had been rejected the previous October, Jackson was an unlikely candidate for the role of civil rights martyr – he wasn't even marching the night of the Marion riot -- but fate has a way of intervening in unpredictable ways, in this case thrusting upon Jackson a mantle he hadn't sought and condemning him to death for a fight he didn't start. As one local activist says, he was simply in the wrong place at the wrong time.

Like much of the Marion police rampage, it isn't clear exactly what happened to Jackson that night. Individual stories differ on certain details, and the official police report was a hastily concocted whitewash designed more to justify the shooting that led to Jackson's death than to determine what actually happened. However, enough eyewitness accounts exist to fashion a reasonably accurate understanding of what transpired amid the chaos.

Jackson had taken his mother, Viola, and his grandfather, Cager Lee, to the Zion United Methodist Church meeting earlier that night and returned later, intending to pick them up. As a black bystander, Jackson was vulnerable to the indiscriminate beatings being perpetrated by the troopers and their posse. So too was Lee, who was attacked despite his age.

Lee recounts: "I was at the back of the church. The men with clubs come around saying, 'Nigger go home.' They hauled me off and hit me and knocked me to the street and kicked me. It was hard to take for an old man whose bones are dry like cane."

He continued: "One of them knew me. He say, 'Why that's Cager. What are you doing here, Cager?' and they let me up.[2]

Wandering through the crowd, Lee found Jackson, who told him he was looking for his mother. "He said he was trying to get (everyone) together to go home," Lee said.

As violence swirled around them, Jackson and Lee sought refuge in Mack's Café, where they hoped to find Viola. By then, many of the fleeing marchers, unable to re-enter the church, had also descended on the café in search of refuge.

Together, Jackson and his elderly grandfather entered the café. Viola Jackson was there, as was Jackson's 17-year-old sister, Emma Jean.

But the troopers weren't far behind. "They came in, saying, 'If you don't live here, get out,'" Viola Jackson told a *New York Times* reporter. Jackson's grandfather, still bleeding from the blow to his head, managed to flee, but when Jackson and his family tried to leave, they were forced back inside by troopers who burst into the café and began swinging their clubs, smashing light fixtures and sending glass shards flying through the room.

Jackson again tried to leave with his family but was wrestled to the floor by troopers who began hitting and kicking him. "They started to whip him up pretty bad," said Albert Turner. Viola Jackson took a drink bottle and tried to force the troopers off her son, but she too was subdued.

"Two of them hit me on my head," she said. "They knocked me down and started beating me on the floor."[3]

When Jimmie Lee leaped up to protect his mother, a trooper grabbed him and pinned him against a cigarette machine. A second trooper, subsequently identified as James Bonard Fowler, drew his revolver and shot Jackson twice in the stomach. A witness, Jeff Moore Jr., told FBI investigators he heard one trooper ask, "Who got him?" and another answer, "I got him."[4]

Jackson was clubbed again as he staggered outside, and lay wounded in the street for half an hour. Another witness, Charles Edward Pryor, said:

> *"I left the café and went about 50 feet and stopped. I looked back and saw several state troopers chasing Jimmie Lee Jackson towards me. Jackson fell to the ground near corner of the church. Several state troopers kicked Jackson and hit*

> *him while he was on the ground. There were many troopers standing around him. Jackson got up and ran around the corner of the church to the post office. State troopers caught him again and the last I saw he was on the ground."*[5]

Jackson himself told FBI investigators he felt he had to leave the cafe to take Cager Lee to the hospital for treatment of the head injuries he sustained during the melee. The official report, dated February 26, 1965, continues:

> *"Jackson stated he had been drinking a Coke in Mack's Cafe after returning and saw a state trooper hitting his mother. He recalled having a Coke bottle in his hand, but does not recall throwing the bottle. He does recall being held back by his sister, Emma Jackson, as he was going to assist his mother. He does recall being close to the door leading to the dance hall when a state trooper shot him in the stomach. He did not fall but immediately ran out of Mack's Café and recalls being hit by troopers with their clubs several times until he was finally stopped in front of the bus station."*[6]

Norma Reen Shaw, the manager of Mack's Café, said she told the first troopers on the scene that there were no problems at the café, but they began forcing black patrons into the back kitchen as well as the dance hall area. After Jackson was shot, she said, a state trooper ordered her and everyone else out of the cafe. He also took her key to the building, telling her he would lock up when it was over.

Checking back the next day, Shaw found the door unlocked and a section of wallboard missing from behind where Jackson had been standing.[7]

Shortly after 10 p.m., Jackson was taken to Perry County Hospital in Marion, where his wounds were cleaned and treated by Dr. Arthur Wilkerson. Wilkerson wanted to open the wound and remove the bullet but was unable to do so because the hospital didn't have a blood bank, and the technician who would typically draw blood from donors was unavailable. He determined that Jackson should be moved to a facility better equipped to treat him, and telephoned for an ambulance.[8]

A hospital employee, Leeandrew Benson, said he saw Jackson lying on a stretcher in the hall. Benson didn't converse with Jackson but heard him say, "I've been shot. Don't let me die."[9]

Minutes later, Jackson was on his way to Good Samaritan Hospital in Selma, along with his mother and grandfather. Ambulance driver Robert Tubbs heard Jackson say only one thing during the ride to Selma, "Lord, save me," which he repeated throughout the trip. Viola Jackson and Cager Lee were treated for their head wounds and released. Jimmie Lee remained hospitalized.[10]

At the Perry County Hospital, meanwhile, Benson was leaving work with a friend, Hardis Jackson (no relation to Jimmie Lee), sometime between 11:30 and 11:45 p.m. Three Alabama state troopers came out the front door several yards behind them. Hardis Jackson heard one of the troopers say, "When I saw blood, I tried to kill the son of a bitch." He assumed the troopers were talking about the shooting of Jimmie Lee Jackson.[11]

Benson confirmed that account, telling investigators that one of the troopers said, "I tried to kill that black bastard when I looked up and saw my blood."[12]

Four days later, Colonel Lingo of the state police strode into Good Samaritan Hospital with a warrant in his hand. He read aloud the state's charges against Jackson: assault and battery with intent to murder a police officer.

Jackson's niece, Julia Greene Cash, recalls turning on the television news the next day, where she saw Jimmie Lee lying in a hospital bed. "They said, 'He's been shot.'"

"I will always remember him trying to sit up in bed, but he just laid back down," Cash added. "I said, 'That's Jimmie!' and the next thing I knew, he was gone."

Governor Wallace reacted to the Marion violence by ordering a ban on nighttime marches. "This action is taken under the police power of the state and is for the purpose of safeguarding all the people of affected areas." He blamed the riot on "career and professional agitators with pro-Communist affiliations."[13]

To no one's surprise, police investigative reports, completed and filed within days of the riot, absolved the troopers and city officers of any responsibility for the violence. A report filed by Major W. R. Jones of the Alabama Department of Public Safety, said it was clear that the people inside the church had been "preached into an emotional frenzy" and were "shouting, singing and clapping hands in a highly excited manner." For that, they blamed C. T. Vivian, who, the report said, "is known to be affiliated with at least one Communist Front group and has at one time been an identified member of the Communist Party." Vivian, the report added, "is probably the most radical member of the SCLC Staff and is known to be a person who advocates and incites violence."

Jones' report also took the marchers to task for "pushing, shouting and striking at officers." The Jackson shooting was dispensed with in two brief sentences: "A Negro male believed to be James Jackson, 26, of Marion, Alabama, struck trooper Frank Higginbotham on the forehead, resulting in his receiving 11 stitches. During the ensuing scuffle, Jackson suffered a gunshot wound in the stomach, fled the cafe, ran up the street and turned in front of the church before being stopped."

Buttressing his case against the protesters, Jones again targeted "outside agitators" who are "especially adept at creating hatred and disrespect for police authority in general." He added: "The Negro agitators have constantly made inflammatory remarks about police authority and on many occasions have presented outright lies concerning contact with police officers. This indoctrination and propaganda closely parallels the Communist Party line with regard to police authority."

In an interesting twist, Jones and Marion Police Chief Harris suggested that the police violence was necessary *for the safety of the black protesters.* Harris contended that Perry County's white residents were becoming rebellious because they thought the police department and sheriff's office, by allowing previous marches, were yielding to the black residents and the so-called outside agitators. He said he was afraid the whites would take matters into their own hands if police didn't respond forcefully.

"It is the writer's opinion," Jones said, "that if law enforcement had broken down, the people would have taken over and there would have been a race riot of major proportions."

Jones concluded that "outside radicals and agitators" deliberately influenced and induced Perry County blacks into a situation where violence and personal injury were inevitable.[14]

Unhappy with the slanted reports from the Alabama State Police and Marion City Police, the U.S. Justice Department wanted an FBI investigation that was thorough and accurate. FBI Director J. Edgar Hoover, who zealously protected his domain and chafed when anyone challenged his authority, must have thrown a private fit upon reading a lengthy memo from John Doar, assistant U.S. Attorney General in charge of the Civil Rights Division, setting forth specific points to be covered in the investigation.

In the February 27 memo, Doar gave Hoover a list of people to be interviewed and specific questions that had to be asked. He also asked for specific details and background information. Doar's memo concluded, "It is requested that all available photographs of these events be obtained.... and all documentary evidence be described (furnish copies if possible) ..."[15]

The memo read like an instructional guide written for a rookie cop with no investigative experience. But if Hoover was offended, as is likely, he didn't tip his hand but instead passed Doar's memo along to the FBI's Alabama office with the curt observation that it was "self-explanatory" and "does not in any way alter their initial request for investigation in this matter, but sets forth more specific information and evidence needed for possible prosecution."

Regardless, notice had been served. The Johnson administration would be watching the investigation closely.

Though the number of people injured that night will never be known because so many – like Preston Hornbuckle and his friend David Herd – sought their own treatment despite suffering serious injuries, an unofficial count reveals that at least 15 people, all marchers, were treated at Good Samaritan Hospital in Selma, mostly for head injuries, bruises and lacerations. Two other marchers, along with state trooper Frank Higginbotham and NBC's Valeriani, were treated for injuries at Perry County Hospital in Marion.

In his report, meanwhile, Chief Harris said many of the marchers' injuries were unintentionally self-inflicted, saying, "Some of them were hurt by themselves and others in the effort to cause them to go back to the church."

On February 21, 1965, three days after a major eruption of violence in his community that resulted in dozens of injuries to town residents and at least one police shooting incident, Marion Police Chief Harris concluded his report: "This case is closed."

The next day, King, who had been bed-ridden in Atlanta for a few days while fighting illness and exhaustion, returned to Selma. In addition to leading a peaceful march, he visited the hospitalized Jimmie Lee Jackson. There is no record of what the two discussed.

In a stunning development, Jackson, who had appeared to be on the way to recovery, died five days later on February 26, officially becoming the first person to be killed in an SCLC campaign. His death was attributed to "massive internal infection" stemming from the gunshot wounds. But like everything associated with Jimmie Lee Jackson, there are more questions than answers.

Dr. William Dinkins, who was one of just two black doctors on staff at Good Samaritan Hospital in Selma in 1965, performed the initial surgery – which he called an exploratory laparotomy – and said Jackson was recovering nicely. A week after the surgery, Dinkins said, Jackson was "sitting up in bed and talking with the nurses and talking with me."

He added, "You could hear normal bowel sounds when you put the stethoscope to his abdomen and so I went home to bed, thinking he's fine."

But he wasn't. At least not in the judgment of another doctor – ostensibly more qualified than Dinkins – who had examined Jackson at the behest of the hospital and determined he required additional surgery.

Dinkins argued vehemently against going back in but was overruled by the other doctor, who was white.[16]

Jackson died early on the morning of February 26, shortly after undergoing his second surgery. Sister Michael Ann, Good Samaritan Hospital administrator, said the four-hour operation was performed by Dinkins, who was assisted by a Dr. Stewart, who, she said, had been called in as a consultant.

While hospital officials insisted Jackson's death was caused by infection, Dinkins disagreed. In an interview conducted for the PBS special *Eyes on the Prize*, Dinkins, now deceased, said he believes Jackson died due to a lack of oxygen during his second surgery.

"I saw his blood turn dark," Dinkins recalled. "I called to the anesthetist and said I think you need to put him on 100 percent oxygen for awhile, and the other doctor said I think we need to give him more anesthesia, so he got more anesthesia. And the next thing I knew, he wasn't breathing anymore."

Nearly 15 years after the fact, Dinkins remained adamant in his belief that the second surgery was unnecessary. "In my opinion, on the night of the 26th, Jimmie Jackson was well on the road to recovery," he said. "He was having no problem, no aggravated temperature, nothing to indicate any danger."[17]

"Dr. Stewart" was never interviewed by the FBI.

The night Jimmie Lee Jackson died, James Bevel and Bernard Lafayette paid a visit to the Jackson family shack in rural Marion. Cager Lee, the only other male in the family, kept repeating, "I wish they had taken me instead of the boy."

Bevel asked the old man if he thought the demonstrations should continue, and Lee said, "Oh, yes, Reverend Bevel, of course they should."

"I've got nothing to lose now ... they've taken all I have," he added. "We got to keep going now."

Bevel asked Lee if he would accompany him at the head of a march, and Lee responded, "Yes, Reverend Bevel. I'll walk with you."[18]

Lafayette assumed Bevel was talking about continuing the demonstrations in Marion, but Bevel had something bigger in mind. Driving back to Selma later that night, he told Lafayette he wanted to march to Montgomery to confront the governor.

The next day there was a mass meeting in Selma. Many of those in attendance were seething with anger, and the hostility was palpable. Hoping to defuse the situation, Bevel took his idea public. "I've got something to say to the governor about Jimmie Lee Jackson," he said. "I've got a lot of questions for Governor Wallace about what really happened. So I thought I would walk to Montgomery and tell the governor in person. Mr. Cager Lee has said he's willing to walk with me."

The crowd roared its approval, with many shouting, "Let's go see the governor." Bevel turned to Lafayette and grinned. "Looks like we got us a march," he said.[19]

Years later, Bevel said his intent was to try to refocus the angry crowd on the issue at hand and channel the negative energy into positive action. "I had to get the people back out of the state ... of violence, and out of a state of grief," he said. "If you don't deal with negative violence and grief, it turns into bitterness." He hoped his suggestion – the march – would give people time to think through their resentment and hostility.

King supported the march idea, which Bevel described as a "classical Gandhi strategy." Giving people an honorable means to express their grief by speaking decisively about an issue, Bevel said, prevents a social movement from deteriorating into disorder and chaos.[20]

Whatever the rationale, SCLC leaders felt they had to do something to renew interest in the Alabama campaign. The national media had begun turning its attention elsewhere, as evidenced by a study of NBC's Huntley-Brinkley Reports nightly news show. Selma and Alabama's Black Belt made the report 17 times for a total of 32 minutes from February 1 to February 19, but only 3 times for a total of less than 4 minutes over the next 13 days.[21]

If there were to be a march, it was decided, it would begin in Selma, not Marion, making the distance and the logistics more manageable. That decision didn't set well with the Marion activists, who felt they had a personal stake in the issue.

Indeed, territorial bitterness remains, even 50 years later. "It happened here and we were going to march to Montgomery to tell Governor Wallace that he had killed Jimmie Lee Jackson, but we knew that was too far," said Marion resident Willie Nell Avery. "You had more Perry County residents in that Bloody Sunday march than anyone. We carpooled to Selma, but Selma gets all the recognition."

The entire Selma campaign was devoted to voting rights, but make no mistake, Avery said, "Bloody Sunday was because of Jimmie Lee Jackson."

Avery is quick to note that Perry County residents aren't necessarily looking for more acclaim, but adds, "The trail should start here."

Albert Turner, Jr., the son of the noted civil rights leader, agrees. Turner is a veteran Perry County board member who continues to advocate aggressively for the area's black residents. "Selma had nothing to do with the march to Montgomery," he said. "It all originated in Marion and the struggles that were going on in Marion."

Chapter 11: Planning the march

The Marion case wasn't closed, at least not officially. There was still the matter of the FBI investigation, but movement leaders didn't have much hope for that either, given Hoover's well-known antipathy toward civil rights leaders, many of whom he suspected of being communists.

Much planning remained to be done, most notably for the proposed march to Montgomery, but first, Jimmie Lee Jackson had to be buried.

Some 400 people crammed into the Zion United Methodist Church on Wednesday, March 3, for the emotional funeral service, and 600 more waited outside on a cold and blustery morning. King and Bevel both spoke at the service, with the typically composed King becoming emotional as he began his eulogy.

His voice cracking, King said there was plenty of blame to share for Jackson's death, from hateful segregationists to the timidity of the federal government, and from the passive response of the moderate masses to the "cowardice" of every black who refused to participate in the struggle for justice. He concluded, "Jimmie Lee Jackson is speaking to us from the casket, and he is saying to us that we must substitute courage for caution ... We must not be bitter, and we must not harbor ideas of revenge."[1]

Virtually the entire black population of Marion came out to pay tribute to Jackson, walking solemnly behind the hearse on the way to the cemetery as a chilling rain fell. Following the service, King flew to New York to meet with advisors, while Bevel announced that the charismatic leader would return Sunday, March 7, to lead a 54-mile march to Montgomery.

Bevel's march plan had been endorsed by King and his SCLC associates, but SNCC leaders, with the exception of John Lewis, strongly opposed the march in the belief that it would help King more than it would help Selma. They feared King and his SCLC colleagues would get a lot of publicity for the huge march and then move on to other campaigns, leaving SNCC workers behind to deal with an inflamed white population.

SNCC Executive Director Jim Forman and others on the board instead proposed intensifying the efforts in Selma, but King and the SCLC were convinced the time had arrived for a dramatic statement, something that would focus national attention on the denial of voting rights. The small-town demonstrations, they felt, had run their course.

Once again putting principle above organizational politics, Lewis noted that the people of the area were hurting and angry and needed to march. "It didn't matter to me who led it," he said years later. "They *needed* to march."[2]

By supporting the march, Lewis had alienated himself from his SNCC colleagues, including top aides Forman and Courtland Cox. He was emotionally torn. Personally, he favored the march, but as SNCC chairman he felt obligated to represent the wishes of the organization. Thus, Lewis had a ready response when Bevel formally announced on March 3 that a Selma-Montgomery march would be held March 7. In a letter to King, he wrote:

"We strongly believe the objectives of the march do not justify its dangers...consequently, the Student Nonviolent Coordinating Committee will only live up to those minimal commitments ... to provide radios and cars, doctors and nurses, and nothing beyond that."[3]

However, Lewis still wanted to march, feeling that failure to do so would be tantamount to abandoning the people of Selma, the people he had worked so closely with over the past three years. Meeting in Atlanta, Lewis told the SNCC executive board, "I'm a native Alabaman. I grew up in Alabama. I feel a deep kinship with the people there on a lot of levels. You know, I've been to Selma many, many times. I've been arrested there. I've been jailed there. I'm going to march with them. You decide what you want to do, but I'm going to march." After a long and rancorous debate, the SNCC board gave permission to Lewis to march, but only as a private citizen, not a SNCC representative.[4]

The fissure between the SCLC and SNCC had become a chasm, as had the fissure within SNCC itself. Younger black leaders, most of them from the North, had been replacing original SNCC members, and while many brought renewed energy to the movement, they also brought an edgier, more ideological approach that was slowly peeling the organization away from its religious roots. These new organizers were less patient than the old guard and lacked the historical perspective of their predecessors, leaving them less inclined to defer to movement elders. The strength of their commitment to nonviolent protest was also being questioned.

In his biography, *Walking with the Wind,* Lewis wrote: "I never imagined my own organization, SNCC, would ever step aside and tell me to walk alone. I would be walking with the people, but my people – the people of SNCC – would not be with me. The fact that those two could ever be separated – the people and SNCC – was something I never imagined."

Lewis's decision to go his own way on the march issue, as well as his cordial relationship with the SCLC, contributed to his defeat when SNCC elected officers the following year. Stokely Carmichael was voted in as chairman, formalizing SNCC's slow but steady drift toward a more radical agenda.

SNCC was polarized, and Lewis was acting too much like Martin Luther King at a time when many of its members were demanding something else. His goal of desegregating public facilities seemed quaintly out of date, as did his belief in the value of integration. By this time, many African-Americans were pursuing the concept of black nationalism, which was abhorrent to Lewis. But nothing symbolized the split as much as Lewis's unyielding faith in the philosophy of nonviolence.

Many SNCC staffers had begun to openly challenge the value of non-violent protest. Carmichael, in fact, would later claim that SNCC had always viewed non-violence as a tactic, not a principle. "The overwhelming majority of people in SNCC never saw non-violence as a philosophy as did those in the SCLC," he said. "For SNCC, it was just a tactic. If it could work, fine. If it can't work, we'll try something else." As early as 1963, he said, most SNCC field staffers were carrying guns.[5]

Meanwhile, Governor Wallace announced that he would prevent the march "by whatever measures are necessary," claiming he could not ensure the safety of the marchers. And the SCLC, despite having already announced the march and solicited volunteers, was beginning to rethink its position. The organization's leaders debated options, with some in favor of postponing the march until a court order providing legal authority could be obtained and others wanting to march regardless and either turn back peacefully when stopped or stand firm and provoke another mass arrest.[6]

Sources differ as to what important decisions were – or weren't – made the day before the march. Some say late Saturday night King ordered the march postponed until Monday and clearly communicated that decision to his subordinates. Others contend the matter was deliberately left unresolved until Sunday, the scheduled day of the march, when march leaders were to assess the situation on the ground before making a call. In effect, they said, it was to be a game-time decision.

******

Sunday morning dawned damp and chilly in Selma. Dark gray clouds drifted ominously overhead. There were already some 500 marchers milling about when Lewis arrived at Brown Chapel at about 12:30 p.m. He immediately sensed something was wrong. A few SCLC staffers were busy training marchers how to protect themselves if they were attacked, but Bevel and Hosea Williams were engaged in an animated conversation with Andrew Young.

Young was berating the two organizers for ignoring what he said was King's decision late the day before to postpone the march until Monday. King, he said, felt that he had missed too much time tending to his own church in Atlanta and felt he had to be there to preach on Sunday and therefore had officially pushed the launch back a day.

Clearly upset, Bevel and Williams argued that the marchers were already on hand and ready to go. The group included a large contingent of Marion residents bused in by Albert Turner. There was no way to turn back now, they said. Besides, Williams argued, any decision King might have made the night before had been rescinded once he realized "how well I got this thing organized."[7]

As usual, Williams was rambunctious, fearless, and blunt. A hard-charging organizer, Williams originally worked for the NAACP but later joined the SCLC and played an important role in the demonstrations in St. Augustine, Florida, that were critical to passage of the landmark Civil Rights Act of 1964. King referred to Williams as "my wild man" and "my bull in a china closet." Williams was always ready to move and would become frustrated when he thought others were over-analyzing a problem.[8]

Young was incredulous over Williams' brazenness, but he also recognized the group was facing a huge problem that had to be solved quickly. To proceed might be to defy King's wishes, but delaying the highly anticipated march would seriously damage the SCLC's credibility and curtail the movement's momentum. Young checked with Bevel, who confirmed Williams' version of events.

Further discussion and a telephone call to King, who had to be summoned from his pulpit at Ebenezer Baptist to take the call, sealed the deal. King reauthorized the march. Upon hearing the news, Williams proclaimed, "We're gone!"

The march would have co-leaders. Lewis was one and King instructed Young to pick one of the three senior SCLC representatives at the scene – Young, Bevel or Williams – as the second. The other two would remain behind to take care of any emergencies.

The three men decided to flip a coin for the right to lead the march with Lewis. The odd man out would be the winner. Young and Bevel flipped tails; Williams flipped heads. A quarter had thus determined the leadership for the most important march in the history of the civil rights movement.[9]

Lewis made a brief statement to the assembled reporters explaining the purpose of the march, and Young then led the entire contingent in prayer. Calling for everyone to kneel, Young said, "As we go through a wilderness of state troopers, go with us."

It was nearly 4 p.m. when the group finally stepped off, walking two abreast, eastward toward the Edmund Pettus Bridge, which would carry marchers over the Alabama River to Highway 80, the road to Montgomery.

Chapter 12: "Troopers, advance!"

Alabama Gov. George Wallace, elected in 1962 largely on his promise of "Segregation now; segregation tomorrow; segregation forever," had inserted himself into the national civil rights debate on June 11, 1963, when he stood in the "school house door" at the University of Alabama in a highly orchestrated event intended to highlight his opposition to the anticipated enrollment of two black students.

Frequently lampooned as a semi-literate backwoods redneck, and known nationally as an inveterate racist, Wallace was in fact a cagey politician who preached a consistent message of social conservatism and economic populism that resonated with many Americans, not just those from Alabama or other southern states. He was smart enough to temper his segregation message with denunciations of race-related violence and was always careful to frame the civil rights debate not as a racial issue but as a matter of states' rights vs. heavy-handed federal government intervention.

The pugnacious, cigar-chomping governor, took particular delight in enumerating the employment gains Alabama blacks had made during his tenure and in skewering northern politicians and reporters for neglecting racial strife in their own communities. Still, Wallace knew whence his real political strength derived and was careful not to allow himself to be out-flanked to the right on the issue of segregation.

Wallace had learned a valuable lesson on race during his failed 1958 bid for the governorship. Running that year against Wallace, then a circuit judge, was state Attorney General John Patterson, a moderate on race who had earlier signed the southern attorneys general resolution denouncing the Ku Klux Klan. Patterson recognized early on that the campaign would turn on race due largely to concerns over *Brown v. Board of Education,* the Supreme Court's school desegregation ruling of 1955, and veered sharply to the right, positioning himself as a staunch segregationist. He even went so far as to seek – and receive – the endorsement of the Ku Klux Klan.

While Patterson was hammering the segregation issue to the exclusion of almost everything else, Wallace diluted his message by discussing issues such as education and roadwork. Despite his innate understanding of the state and its residents, Wallace realized too late that in mid-century Alabama, race wasn't the biggest issue, it was the only issue.[1]

"I started off talking about schools and prisons and highways and taxes, and I couldn't make them listen" he said. "Then I began talking about niggers and they stomped the floor."[2]

Wallace lost in a close election, and reportedly vowed to never be "out-niggered" again. As if to prove the point, he borrowed his infamous "Segregation now!" pledge from a Klan proclamation declaring that they would ride "yesterday, today, forever" as long as white men lived.

Skillfully playing the powerful race card, Wallace easily defeated moderate attorney Ryan DeGraffenried in the 1962 race for governor. One of his first moves as governor was to replace State Safety Commissioner Floyd Mann, who had protected the Freedom Riders, with Al Lingo, a big, burly man and avowed racist who had served as Wallace's personal pilot during the campaign.[3]

Even at this early stage, Wallace had national political ambitions and was wary of appearing too overtly racist. He thus shuffled the deck and pulled out a new race card, one that emphasized states' rights and attacks on liberal government, while avoiding conspicuous bigotry.

Many of Wallace's anti-Washington themes and conservative platitudes were embedded with racial catch-phrases that advanced his real platform under the polite cover of acceptable public discourse. One Alabama lawmaker said at the time, "He can use all the other issues – law and order, running your own schools, protecting property rights – and never mention race. But people will know he's telling them, 'A nigger's trying to get your job, trying to move into your neighborhood.' What Wallace is doing is talking to them in a kind of shorthand, a kind of code."[4]

This approach, refined and tempered, became known as the "Southern strategy" and would subsequently be used to great effect by future President Richard Nixon in his 1968 and 1972 campaigns.

Like Wallace, Nixon had suffered an earlier defeat due at least in part to his failure to grasp the racial animosity of many white southerners. During his failed 1960 run for president, Nixon had insisted on a Republican Party platform plank that went farther in support of civil rights than many of his conservative supporters would have liked. Aligning himself with the moderate wing of the Party, as embodied by New York Gov. Nelson Rockefeller, Nixon likely supported the plank as a matter of both conscience and tactics. He truly believed in civil rights. However, he also believed that the black vote in northern cities would be more critical to his success than the southern white vote and thus rejected a non-committal plank presented by the GOP Platform Committee that deliberately avoided any outright declaration of support for black sit-in strikes at southern lunch counters and omitted any promise of federal intervention to secure and protect civil rights.[5]

Nixon had to weigh the value of the northern black vote against the white support he likely would lose in the South due to his moderate stance, and ultimately decided it was a beneficial trade-off. In his view, the Republicans would match the Democrats in support of racial reforms instead of re-orienting the party toward an axis of Northern-Southern conservatives.

Although morally sound, Nixon's decision was politically disastrous. The original plank would almost certainly have carried the southern states for him, guaranteeing a Republican victory, but Nixon's more liberal rewrite drained valuable southern votes away from his ticket, and John Kennedy's Democrats hung on to win Texas, Arkansas, Louisiana, Georgia and South Carolina.

Nothing if not a shrewd political tactician, Nixon would not make that same mistake in subsequent campaigns when he vigorously employed a conservative southern strategy calling for the preservation of state sovereignty that not only assisted in his election but destroyed the Democratic Party's once secure grip on the Deep South.

In 1968, a united South froze out the Democrats by supporting Wallace's independent candidacy for president, and in 1972, the South, along with most of the rest of the nation voted for Nixon.

But while Wallace might have been privately harboring national aspirations in 1965, events in Alabama demanded his full attention. Through most of the Selma campaign, Wallace had remained silent, trusting Lingo to keep him apprised of developments. But the stakes had now been raised. With marchers about to embark on a highly visible and dangerous intrastate trek, it was time for the governor to engage.[6]

Saturday morning, Wallace called a news conference to announce that the march proposed for the next day would not be tolerated. In prohibiting the march, he cited potential disruptions to "the orderly flow of traffic and commerce" and the "additional hazards placed on highway travel."

Wallace said he had instructed Lingo to "use whatever measures necessary to prevent a march" but later contended that was a deliberate exaggeration designed to deter the marchers.

Wallace and Lingo met again Saturday night, this time with Sheriff Clark. A Wallace aide said they left the governor's office with a clear understanding of the ground rules: not to do anything more than hold their nightsticks in front of them and let the marchers through if they pushed ahead. Wallace also claims he told the troopers to give the marchers a chance to disperse peacefully before using tear gas.[7]

In retrospect, the indecisiveness and communication gaffes from both sides likely ensured the disaster that was about to unfold, but neither side could gracefully back down. The event was lurching forward, with both sides bedeviled by serious misunderstandings and a troubling lack of clarity. A Birmingham reporter, Tom Lankford, later wrote: "It was like something rehearsed and predestined, the actors manipulated by unseen forces."[8]

******

Led by Lewis and Williams, the protesters, about 600 strong, marched quietly and peacefully from Brown Chapel toward the Edmund Pettus Bridge, a span of about four blocks. Directly behind the two march leaders were Amelia Boynton of the Dallas County Voters League, and Bob Mants of SNCC, who insisted on marching out of loyalty to Lewis.

It was a somber and subdued group, almost funereal. No one was jostling or pushing to get ahead. "There was no singing, no shouting," Lewis said in his autobiography. "Just the sound of scuffling feet. There was something holy about it, as if we were walking down a sacred path."

Charles Bonner, a young SNCC volunteer, was frightened. Bonner was a protest veteran, and he could tell there was something different about this march. "We had the uneasiness that this was going to be a different day," he said. "Frankly it was a fear. It was a terror that was going through us all. We were scared, because we didn't know what was going to happen."[9]

Arriving at the apex of the bridge, those in front were confronted by a sea of blue. Just east of the bridge were 25 state troopers in full riot gear lined up shoulder to shoulder across the divided, four-lane highway. Behind them were another 75 troopers and a posse of more than 30 deputies, about half of whom were mounted. It was a battle-ready group armed with guns, billy clubs, tear gas canisters, and, for the posse members, baseball bats.

Selma police officers were not part of the amassed force. Safety Director Baker, fearing that Lingo and Clark would escalate the Sunday confrontation, had told Mayor Smitherman on Saturday night that he would not let his officers participate. A compromise was reached Sunday morning in which it was agreed that city officers would neither arrest the marchers before they reached the troopers' blockade just east of town, as Baker preferred, nor give aid to the troopers and Clark's posse if and when a confrontation erupted. Baker's officers would be in charge of all police activities when the marchers crossed back over the bridge to the city.

Lewis and Williams brought the line to a halt as they surveyed the scene. After a brief pause, the marchers proceeded cautiously, their hearts beating louder, their breathing a bit more labored. Glancing at the churning water of the Alabama River 100 feet below, Williams asked Lewis if he could swim.

"No," said Lewis.

"Well," Williams responded, "neither can I. But we might have to."[10]

As the distance between the two sides diminished, a state trooper stepped forward to identify himself. He said, "I'm Major John Cloud. This is an unlawful march. I'll give you two minutes to disperse and go back to your church."

"May we have a word with the major?" Williams asked.

"There is no word to be had," Cloud responded.

Lewis was determined not to turn back. "We were there. We weren't going to run," he explained later. Indeed, the lengthy line of people would have made it exceedingly difficult to turn back even if that were the decision. But nor did he or Williams want to march directly into the blue wall of troopers, an option they considered too provocative.

Lewis suggested that they kneel and pray, and Williams quickly agreed. But Major Cloud was growing impatient. As the marchers began kneeling to pray, Cloud barked out his command: *"Troopers, advance!"* It was one minute since he had issued his warning.[11]

Having anticipated Cloud's order, the troopers responded swiftly and decisively, barreling into the marchers in a frenzy of rage so violent it shocked even those who had feared the worst.

What followed is best described by those who were actually there to observe. William Cook of *Newsweek* magazine reported:

"The 25 troopers formed a flying wedge and started walking forward, picking up speed until, by the time they reached the head of the line, they were nearly running. They rammed into Williams and Lewis, pushing them backwards into the ones behind. The marchers were shoved along, like clothes on hangers pushed along a rod ... they were pushed backward and toppled like dominoes.

"The troopers rushed among the Negroes, flailing wildly with their clubs, knocking heads, as the crowd screamed. 'God, we're being killed,' someone shouted. 'Please, no!' another cried. Sheriff Clark's cavalry charged in, scattering more people. Then, the troopers moved in again and discharged tear gas. It billowed in a low, blue-gray cloud. Over the top of the cloud, billy clubs could be seen, thrashing the Negroes.

"Amelia Boynton lay sprawled on the turf ... Through all this, the whites on the south side of the highway were cheering and clapping."[12]

And Roy Reed of the *New York Times* said:

"The wedge of troopers moved with such force that it seemed almost to pass through the waiting column instead of into it. The first 15 or 20 marchers were swept to the ground, screaming, arms and legs flying ... Those still on their feet retreated.

"The troopers continued pushing,

using both the force of their bodies and the prodding of their nightsticks. The mounted possemen spurred their horses and rode at a run into the retreating mass. The Negroes cried out as they crowded together for protection, and the whites on the sideline whooped and cheered.

"Suddenly there was a report like a gunshot and a gray cloud spewed over the troopers and the Negroes.

"'Tear gas!' someone yelled."[13]

Volunteer Lafayette Surrey, speaking live to SNCC offices in Atlanta over a wide area telephone service (WATS) line, reported the following:

> *4:15 p.m. – State troopers are throwing tear gas at the people. A few are running back. A few are being blinded by tear gas. Somebody has been hurt ... I don't know who ... They're beating them and throwing tear gas at them.*
>
> *4:16 p.m.—Police are beating people on the streets. Oh, man, they're just picking them up and putting them in ambulances. People are getting hurt pretty bad. There were two people on the ground in pretty bad shape ... I'm going to leave in a few minutes. People are running back this way.*
>
> *4:17 p.m. – Ambulances are going by with their sirens going. People are running, crying, telling what's happening.*
>
> *4:18 p.m. -- Police are pushing people into alleys. I don't know why. People are screaming, hollering. They're bringing in more ambulances. People are running, hollering, crying ...*
>
> *4:20 p.m. – Here come the white hoodlums. I'm on the corner of one of the main streets. One lady screamed, "They're trying to kill me."*

4:26 p.m. – They're going back to the church. I'm going too ... [14]

Lewis was knocked unconscious. Although he didn't know it at the time, he had a fractured skull. When he came to, he saw mayhem all around -- a young boy with blood streaming from a gash in his head, several women lying in the pavement, people crying and vomiting from the tear gas.

The initial encounter of what immediately became known as "Bloody Sunday" lasted 18 minutes.

Black marchers began retreating back across the bridge to Brown Chapel, leaving the ground behind strewn with caps, purses, umbrellas, sleeping bags, and shoes. It looked like an abandoned battlefield.

At this time, many of the white onlookers rushed in, attacking cameramen and reporters, and chasing marchers back toward the downtown area. Clark and his posse pursued the stragglers back over the bridge, clubbing those who attempted to dash for the chapel or a nearby house. A new round of violence erupted just blocks from Brown Chapel, this one led by Clark, not Major Cloud.

Clark and his men continued their pursuit right up to the chapel, which had been hastily converted into a makeshift MASH unit. Marchers lay on the floor and chairs, many weeping and moaning. A young girl was carried from the building, screaming.[15]

Baker, furious that Clark had violated the policing agreement by pursuing marchers back into the city, arrived on the scene and confronted the sheriff, demanding that he and his men retreat. The two men glared at one another for a moment until Clark and his posse pulled back.

Clark would later claim that Baker wasn't tough enough for his job and was in fact aligned with King. "Wilson Baker went along with the wishes of Martin Luther King and the other outside agitators that came in," he told an interviewer. "I don't think anybody of that caliber should be in the office of director of public safety."

Ambulances dispatched by black funeral homes shuttled injured marchers from the chapel to Good Samaritan Hospital and the Burwell Infirmary. More than 90 people were treated for broken bones, deep head gashes, and fractured ribs, 17 of whom required hospitalization.[16]

As the shock of the attack began to wear off, hundreds of blacks, many of whom had taken part in the march, milled about angrily in front of the chapel. Some threw bricks and rocks at the assembled troopers and possemen. Black leaders walked through the crowd, urging restraint.

Meanwhile, national Sunday night television programming was disrupted as all three networks showed footage from that day's riots. ABC interrupted *Judgment at Nuremberg,* a film about Nazi war crimes, to show Alabama police attacking American citizens. The irony did not escape many viewers, most of whom were appalled to see defenseless men, women and children being brutally beaten because of the color of their skin.

The *New York Times,* like most every other paper in the country, played the Selma violence story at the top of Page 1 with the bold banner headline, "Alabama Police Use Gas and Clubs to Rout Negroes."

The *Selma Times-Journal* took a decidedly more circumspect approach, playing the story nearly half-way down the page with the innocuous headline, "Civil Rights Leader Will Seek Sanction of Court for March." Stories deemed more significant than the violence, which occurred literally in the back yard of the *Times-Journal* building, were "Return Fire

By Marines Given Force by Rusk," "Soviet Embassy Target of Cuban Bottle Hurling," and the top story of the day, "Johnson Asks Congress To Intensify Fight On Crime."[17]

Most of the nation held Wallace responsible for the attack, but the governor publicly insisted the state had saved lives by halting the march, contending "there's a good possibility that death would have resulted to some of those people if we had not stopped them."[18]

Privately, Wallace is said to have been furious with Lingo for ignoring his orders to avoid the use of force.

Many of the shocked marchers remained at Brown Chapel late into the evening, rehashing the day's events and debating the future of the campaign. Rumbles about armed retaliation were growing louder. It was a dispirited, demoralized group. But help was already on the way.

Chapter 13: Turnaround Tuesday

In the immediate aftermath of the Bloody Sunday violence, King pointed an accusing finger at Wallace for failing to prevent troopers from "degenerating to the lowest form of barbarity." He announced that he would seek federal legal approval for a follow-up march he intended to lead on Tuesday, just two days hence, and called on religious leaders and supporters from across the country to join the marchers.

Response was instantaneous, which encouraged the beleaguered marchers still trying to make sense of things at Brown Chapel. At about 11 p.m. Sunday, as those marchers still on hand debated the wisdom of continuing the campaign, the doors of the church swung open. In came a group of people from New Jersey, black and white, who had chartered a plane as soon as they heard that day's news out of Selma.

Said the voters league's Frederick Reese: "They walked into the church, down the aisle, and said to us, 'We are here to share with the people of Selma in this struggle for the right to vote.'"[1]

The church erupted in loud applause. Reese said the change in the atmosphere was palpable, explaining, "You could feel a spirit of inspiration, motivation, hope coming back into the eyes and into the minds of these people."

The folks from New Jersey might have been the first to arrive, but they weren't the last. Literally overnight, hundreds of concerned people poured into Selma intent on doing something to help the cause.

On Monday, SCLC attorneys went to court in Montgomery to petition Federal District Judge Frank M. Johnson Jr. for an order barring state obstruction of Tuesday's march. Johnson was an old college buddy of Wallace's but was generally considered to be fair and reasonable. By virtue of his questions, Johnson seemed inclined to impose the order, which would have given the march much-desired legal sanction, but declined to do so until he heard the anticipated appeals from the state. Instead, Johnson issued two injunctions, one preventing Wallace, Lingo, and Clark from interfering with peaceful demonstrations, and the second forbidding the SCLC from attempting another march until after a hearing he set for March 11.

King was discouraged by Judge Johnson's order delaying and possibly forbidding a second march, saying it was like condemning the robbed man for getting robbed. He also recognized that it put him in the challenging position of having to control a potentially explosive situation while at the same time obeying a federal court order.

Addressing a Monday night mass meeting at Brown Chapel, King attacked the authorities and praised those who had been courageous enough to submit to the Sunday assault without fighting back. He called for unity and then unexpectedly concluded by repeating his announcement that a renewed effort to march to Selma would begin at 1 p.m. the next day. King's words drew lusty applause but came as a surprise to his aides, who said King had intended to announce a delay of the march pending word on the legal injunction but was swept up in the emotion of the moment.[2]

King was now trapped. He had gone too far to turn back, but he also knew that he would not have Judge Johnson's ruling in time for the Tuesday march. Meanwhile, upwards of 2,000 people, many of whom had traveled hundreds of miles to support the cause, were girding for another confrontation, one with the potential to dwarf Sunday's violence.

Movement leaders discussed the dilemma late Monday night and on into Tuesday morning. Tempers flared, but no decisions were made before the participants straggled off to sleep shortly before daybreak. March time was approaching.

After just a few hours of sleep, they were back at it, this time accompanied by Assistant U.S. Attorney General John Doar and another federal government representative. King and the others still could see no way out of their predicament. The options were few and unappealing. They could call off the march until they received a green light from Judge Johnson, which would damage morale and frustrate those who had traveled great distances to take part, or they could proceed in defiance of the order preventing the march, placing themselves on the wrong side of the law and risking another round of violence.

Finally, a compromise plan emerged. King would lead a march over the Pettus Bridge to the spot where blood was shed on Sunday. When stopped by the authorities, they would turn around and walk back across the bridge. It would be a symbolic journey, a mere reenactment of Sunday's march, but would allow the leaders to obey the federal injunction while telling the marchers they had made their point.[3]

Following the harrowing Bloody Sunday march by just two days, and preceded by a flurry of legal maneuvering,

Tuesday's King-led march was shaping up to be anti-climactic at best, and an orchestrated charade at worst. In essence, it would be a march not to influence public opinion but to buy time until yet another march could be held. It wouldn't satisfy anyone but might give King and his colleagues enough political cover to maintain unity and keep their forces in line.

King agreed to the plan providing he receive assurances from Lingo and Clark that the police forces would keep their distance and refrain from initiating any violence. The deal was struck over a cup of coffee at the breakfast table, with King and Abernathy still in their pajamas.

Later that morning, King was informed that Lingo and Clark had agreed to the plan. The script was written and now it befell the actors to play their respective roles.

Abernathy's heart sank as he watched the throngs of people headed to Brown Chapel to prepare for the march. As he wrote in *And the Walls Came Tumbling Down*, "They were swarming like a huge invading army, covering the land, the sidewalks and the streets. Under different circumstances my heart would have leapt at the sight of them, but this morning I saw their numbers as a mixed blessing. In an hour's time they might all be shaking their fists at us for having sold them out."[4]

The march began, and everything was proceeding according to plan until Lingo's troopers made a surprise move just before the marchers were to be told to turn back. The troopers retreated to one side, leaving the marchers with an open highway and a straight shot to Montgomery. Not having anticipated this move, King paused and considered his options. While the temptation to proceed must have been great, he quickly determined there was more to be lost than gained by violating the injunction and thus decided to turn back.

The marchers were confused and angry. They had come prepared to sacrifice, to make a difference, and now they were retreating. They followed King back over the bridge, but many were visibly upset. Rev. Orloff Miller of Berkeley, California, a Unitarian minister who marched on what became known as "Turnaround Tuesday," said, "All of a sudden I realized people were turning around and coming back, and I was aghast. It felt just awful. I had come to lay myself on the line just as much as people in Selma had done 48 hours before, and here I was in a turnaround march."[5]

King was forced to admit: "We agreed that we would not break through the lines ... In all frankness, we knew we would not get to Montgomery."[6]

SNCC, long dissatisfied with its subordinate role in Selma, had had enough. Within 24 hours, Executive Director James Forman had shifted SNCC's efforts to Montgomery, where student groups began a series of demonstrations at the capitol. The protests there would prove to be more aggressive than those in Selma, as the marchers openly taunted and provoked law enforcement authorities.[7]

In the wake of Bloody Sunday and Turnaround Tuesday, even the most moderate SNCC members were demanding more aggressive action. They were tired of rules and procedures that left them politically hobbled and physically defenseless. They wanted change, and their hopes were fueled by Carmichael and Forman, who, over the course of the next year, began implementing an even more confrontational approach and promoting a philosophy of black separatism.

Those efforts eventually led to the end of Lewis's reign as SNCC chairman. Lewis was voted out of office in May 1966 during a bitterly contentious meeting of the SNCC board. He was replaced by Stokely Carmichael.

In another sign of the changing times, Carmichael and his colleagues officially created a new political party in Lowndes County, Alabama, adjacent to Dallas County, first called the Lowndes County Freedom Organization, but soon to be known as the Black Panther Party. In time, Black Panther organizations were springing up across the country, some sharing little more than the name and an attitude of open defiance.[8]

Although Abernathy says Lewis was among those angry with King, calling his actions a "sell-out," Lewis himself says he had no problem with the decisions King made. Everyone knew Judge Johnson would lift the injunction within a day or two, he said, and King was wise to follow the rules. When asked at a rally that night about the "split" between SNCC and the SCLC, Lewis said, "I am not going to engage in any public discussion of organizational problems. SCLC is not the problem. George Wallace and segregation are the problem."

Judge Johnson would, in fact, lift the injunction, but not until more violence had erupted, this time deadly.

******

The night of the Turnaround Tuesday march, three white Unitarian ministers entered Walker's Café, a restaurant in the black section of Selma. As they ate, they discussed the day's events, concluding that the march probably hadn't achieved much.

Walker's Cafe was busy that night as civil rights activists, both black and white, shared their experiences with one another. After finishing his meal of fried chicken and mashed potatoes, James Reeb, pastor of a large Boston congregation, called his wife from the restaurant's phone booth. Everything is fine, he told her, we're going to stay one more day.[9]

Paying their bills, the three ministers walked out into the brisk night air, still engaged in conversation. Approaching the end of the block, they were confronted by a small group of young white men wearing windbreakers, one holding a five-foot 2x4. The pastors heard the scream from across the street, *"White niggers!"* Whispering to themselves, they decided to just keep walking. Approaching the pastors from behind, the armed assailant smashed his 2x4 into Reeb's skull. Reeb fell to the ground, struggling to retain consciousness. One of the other pastors had his glasses knocked off. And then, just as quickly, it was over. The men raced off into the night.[10]

Reeb was transported to Birmingham's University Hospital, where brain surgery could be performed. Word filtered back to Selma that Reeb's prognosis was not good, but he managed to cling to life for two days. Late Thursday night, Reeb died without ever regaining consciousness. As author Jim Bishop noted in *The Days of Martin Luther King, Jr.*, "Reeb's last conscious vision was the face of a white man contorted with hate."[11]

Both President Johnson and Vice President Humphrey made calls to the Reeb family. A memorial service was held in Selma, and protests erupted in northern cities. The movement mourned Reeb, but some couldn't help but compare the national outrage with the relative silence following the death of Jimmie Lee Jackson. The tragic irony was that the murder of a white citizen generated more media attention and condemnation of southern racist violence than the deaths of many blacks, including Jackson, in the struggle for civil rights.

Within days, Baker announced the arrests of four men for the murder of James Reeb, but only three were indicted. Two months later, an all-white jury acquitted the three of beating Reeb to death after deliberating for 97 minutes.

Chapter 14: Lyndon Johnson

President Lyndon Johnson, a native of the Texas hill country, the far western edge of the confederacy, was an unlikely champion for civil rights. In fact, his lengthy legislative record suggested just the opposite. First elected to Congress in 1937, Johnson never supported a civil rights bill as a member of the House of Representatives. He voted against anti-lynching bills, opposed legislation to abolish the poll tax, voted against a bill that would have punished schools for racial discrimination, and opposed the idea of a Fair Employment Practices Commission.

In general, his political record was marked by a long history of opposing the federal government's attempts to foster racial integration, which put him in the mainstream of southern political thought.

But there was another side to Johnson, a progressive, more tolerant side. While most of his regional colleagues used racial divisiveness to their political advantage, Johnson never made segregation a central theme of his campaigns and never once discussed the issue of civil rights on the House floor during his 12 years as a congressman.

Though he might have been tempted otherwise, Johnson understood the politics of race and wasn't about to risk his promising career by appearing too progressive too soon. He recognized that to be effective he first had to survive. But he also had a growing conviction that government should do more to help improve the economic and living conditions of blacks and other minorities.[1]

Even early on, Johnson displayed a willingness to help racial and ethnic minorities, albeit quietly and behind the scenes. After obtaining a two-year teaching certificate in 1928, he moved to Cotulla, Texas, south of San Antonio to serve as teacher and principal at a school attended almost exclusively by Mexican-Americans. The living conditions of these students left a lasting impression on the future president.

"They were poor ... and hungry," he recalled years later. "They knew even in their youth the pain of prejudice."

He added: "Somehow you never forget what poverty and hatred can do when you see its scars on the hopeful face of a young child."[2]

Appointed director of the National Youth Administration, a New Deal agency, in 1935, Johnson's work impressed black leaders in Texas and Washington. An energetic young man with big ambitions, Johnson quickly announced a goal to enroll 20,000 Texas youth in school or in work on NYA projects. Although it was omitted from his press release, the fact that he opened the program to all Texas youth, including blacks and Mexican-Americans, did not go unnoticed by minority communities. He also met regularly with black leaders to inform them of his plans and conferred often with presidents of the state's black colleges.[3]

This public/private contradiction would define Johnson throughout his national political career where it manifested itself not just on civil rights but on other major issues, such as the Vietnam War. He was a master politician, often saying one thing in public and doing something totally different in private, and would use every tool at his disposal to bring others around to his point of view.

A big man, Johnson liked to get close to his opponents and tower over them as he sought to make his point. For emphasis, he would stab their chests with a long index finger. No one was immune from the Johnson treatment, which ranged from quiet persuasion embellished by flattery to vehement arm-twisting accompanied by epithet-laden threats. Fellow lawmakers, bureaucrats, staff members and interest groups were all subject to Johnson's charm and/or wrath, sometimes during the same meeting.

As Senate majority leader and later president, Johnson was the picture of self-confidence, supremely sure of his position and eager to bend others to his will, but that too was part of the act. Johnson's public expressions of optimism and private lobbying sessions were often followed by periods of nagging self doubt during which he frequently would confess his fears and insecurities to a trusted adviser.

Over time, Johnson became more open about his desire to help minority communities, and while civil rights leaders discovered early on they could count him as an ally, many still were beset with doubts over his segregationist past. Having assumed the presidency during a time of international crises and the swirling forces of domestic cultural upheaval, Johnson was supportive but also preoccupied with matters other than civil rights. Many movement leaders believed he should have been more attentive to their concerns.

But while he may have been indecisive at times, Johnson was not indifferent, and he was sensitive to intimations that he should be doing more, faster. All along, he had been preparing a new voting rights bill and he had told civil rights leaders on several occasions that he was committed to congressional action on the issue. That, he thought, should have dispelled any doubts as to his intentions, but movement leaders remained wary. "Once again," he lamented later, "my southern heritage was thrown in my face."[4]

History was, in fact, repeating itself. For the second time in a century, an assassinated president had been succeeded by a white southerner entrusted with the Herculean task of solving the nation's racial and regional divisions. In an unpublished draft of his memoirs, Johnson said he felt kinship with "another southerner named Johnson" who had "tried to hold the country together" after his predecessor's murder.[5]

Many black leaders and northern congressmen were imploring Johnson to send federal troops to Alabama, but the president feared the impact that would have on the southern psyche, as well as the southern vote. Despite his outrage over the violence in Selma, Johnson knew he didn't have the luxury of acting impulsively. He understood that passage of landmark voter rights legislation would require a confluence of many positive factors, including timing, public opinion, a deft lobbying touch, and political courage. To overreact now and send uninvited troops to Alabama would threaten the delicate balance he was trying to achieve.

"If I just send federal troops with their big black boots and rifles, it'll look like Reconstruction all over again," he said. "I'll lose every moderate not just in Alabama, but all over the South .... If it looks like the Civil War all over again, that will force them right into the arms of extremists and make a martyr out of Wallace."[6]

But events in Selma had changed the political dynamic, creating a window of opportunity for the White House on voting rights. Johnson knew that window would not remain open indefinitely and was eager to introduce the bill his administration had been working on for months. When others in his administration lobbied for more time, the president pushed back hard. According to Attorney General Nicholas Katzenbach, Johnson said, "Get it and get it now. We have a majority to do it and we can do it."[7]

Without Johnson's tenacious arm-twisting and full-bore lobbying campaign a year earlier, it's unlikely that the Civil Rights Act of 1964 would have been approved. And now the President stood poised to formally introduce legislation the movement wanted more than anything – a comprehensive voting rights act.

First, however, he had to decide what to do about Wallace, who was an unpredictable and potentially volatile presence.

Wallace, meanwhile, was struggling with his own unappealing political alternatives. He was reluctant to use his National Guard – and state dollars -- to protect people campaigning for integration, but to sit back and do nothing was an even more problematic option. Under the first scenario, Wallace would be criticized and politically damaged for aligning himself with the Feds; under the second, he risked being held responsible for any violence that might erupt during the march.

With outrage over Reeb's murder roiling the country and scattered, disorganized protests breaking out in the streets of Montgomery, Johnson was confident he had his adversary trapped and thus decided to wait for Wallace to make the next move. He didn't have to wait long.

On Friday, March 12, Wallace sent a lengthy telegram to the White House suggesting that he and the President might be able to work out a solution to the street demonstrations taking place "in defiance of lawful state and federal authority." Johnson agreed and a meeting was hastily arranged for the next day, Saturday, March 13.

There are no formal minutes of the meeting, which lasted more than hours, but aides for both sides agree that Johnson gave Wallace the full treatment. Greeting him with a crushing handshake, the President guided his guest to a cushy White House sofa and then pulled his own rocking chair uncomfortably close. The two adversaries were literally eye to eye. "Well, governor," Johnson said. "You wanted to see me."

After listening to Wallace complain about "communist agitators" trained in New York or Moscow, and appeal for help in restoring civil order to the streets of Alabama, Johnson drew even closer.

According to a reconstructed account of the meeting prepared by various aides, the conversation grew intense:

Johnson: Wouldn't it be just wonderful if we could put an end to all those demonstrations?

Wallace: Oh, yes, Mr. President, that would be wonderful.

Johnson: Then why don't you let the Negroes vote?

Wallace: They can vote if they're registered.

Johnson: Well, then, George, why don't you just tell them county registrars to register those Negroes?

Wallace: I don't have that power, Mr. President. Under Alabama law, that belongs to the county registrars.

Johnson: George, don't you shit me. Who runs Alabama? Don't shit me about your persuasive powers. I had on the

TV this morning and I saw you and you was attacking me, George.

Wallace: Not you, Mr. President. I was speaking against federal intervention.

Johnson: You was attacking me, George. And you know what? You were so damned persuasive that I almost changed my mind. George, you and I shouldn't be thinking about 1968. We should be thinking about 1988. We'll both be dead and gone then. What do you want left behind? You want a great big monument that says. "George Wallace: He Built"? Or do you want a little piece of scrawny pine that says, "George Wallace: He hated"?[8]

One Johnson aide said Wallace left the meeting twisted up "like a rubber band." Wallace later said, "Hell, if I'd stayed in there much longer, he'd have had me coming out for civil rights."

At the ensuing news conference, Johnson announced he would send voting rights legislation to Congress the next week. He also forcefully denounced the violence in Selma. "It is wrong to do violence to peaceful citizens in the streets of their towns," he said. "It is wrong to deny any person full equality because of the color of his skin."

As Wallace looked on silently, Johnson told reporters that he had "advised the governor of my intention to press with all the vigor at my command to assure that every citizen of this country is given the right to participate in his government at every level through the complete voting process."

But Wallace, having had a night to recover, went on the next morning's news programs to press his case against outside agitators riling up the good people of Alabama.

He was as feisty as ever.

Meanwhile, Johnson had to decide how to introduce his voting rights bill. Counseled by some congressional leaders to take a low-key approach, Johnson, acting on the advice of Vice President Hubert Humphrey, instead decided to send a strong message by presenting the bill himself before a joint session of Congress.

It would be the first time in nearly 20 years that a president would take a legislative message directly to Congress, the last coming on May 25, 1946, when Harry Truman addressed a joint session in regard to a national railroad workers strike.

The next night, Monday, March 15, Johnson exited the White House and slid into the back seat of his armored black limousine, one of four such cars in a motorcade that would make the short trek from the White House to Capitol Hill. Though he was accompanied by several close aides, there was no small talk. Under a small backseat light, Johnson focused intently on his speech, putting his hand out for the next page before he had even finished the one before it. He didn't even glance up as the motorcade glided past demonstrators gathered on a White House sidewalk to protest the administration's perceived inactivity on civil rights.[9]

In a few short minutes, Johnson would be standing at a podium in the House of Representatives, addressing a joint session of Congress and a national television audience about the need for a Voting Rights bill. His aides had never seen him so grimly determined before a major speech.

Word had gone out in Washington that the President had prepared something special, and the closer it got to the speech time, the louder the buzz became. Cabinet members, Supreme Court justices and ambassadors were among those left scrambling for seats in the House chamber. Even the aisles were filled. The jam highlighted the fact that the Mississippi and Virginia congressional delegations and many individual congressmen from other southern states were boycotting the speech.[10]

If Johnson noticed, he didn't seem to care.

The president used the first part of the speech to frame the issue in moral terms. "Rarely in any time does an issue lay bare the secret heart of American itself," he said. "Rarely are we met with a challenge not to our growth or our abundance, our welfare or our security, but rather to the values and purposes and the meaning of our beloved nation."

His demeanor as much as his words alerted those in attendance, as well as those watching at home, that something extraordinary was happening. Johnson was not a naturally gifted public speaker, his typically measured delivery rarely matched the lofty message he was seeking to impart, and this night was no different. If anything, he was speaking slower and more methodically than usual, taking care with every word as if a single mispronunciation or improperly emphasized syllable would detract from his singular focus.

This quietly determined approach, free of histrionics and rhetorical flourishes, was perfect for the occasion. It was as if Johnson were dismayed that such a speech was necessary, and was intent on getting it right to preclude the need for repeat performances. He was placing a significant marker.

Speaking for "the dignity of man and the destiny of democracy," a somber Johnson said, "At times history and fate meet in a single time in a single place to shape a turning point in man's unending search for freedom. So it was at Lexington and Concord. So it was a century ago at Appomattox. So it was last week in Selma, Alabama."

Declaring that the fight for equal rights for black citizens was a mission directly linked to America's most fundamental principles, Johnson said, "There is no Negro problem. There is no southern problem. There is an American problem." Prompting a volley of cheers, he added, "And we are met here tonight as Americans – not as Democrats or Republicans – we are met here as Americans to solve that problem." It was the first of some 40 times the speech would be interrupted by applause.

Johnson was well into the speech before making his first direct reference to voting rights. "Every American must have an equal right to vote," he said. "There is no reason which can excuse the denial of that right. There is no duty which weighs more heavily on us than the duty we have to ensure that right."

A thunderous roar of approval greeted Johnson's assertion that "this time, on this issue, there must be no delay, no hesitation and no compromise with our purpose," but the emotional apex of the speech came when the president paused after calling on all Americans to "help overcome the crippling legacy of bigotry and injustice," and then proceeded to declare: "And ... we ... *shall...* overcome!"

The entire chamber was on its feet, cheering wildly. Many observers wept.[11]

Watching on television, King and several top aides couldn't believe what they were hearing. Cheers mixed with tears as the SCLC leaders celebrated the speech, especially Johnson's decision to co-opt a phrase that was synonymous with the civil rights movement.

By making the language of the movement his own, Johnson shattered any lingering doubts about unity of purpose. The President would stand with the marchers. Johnson didn't ask for support in this cause so much as he *demanded* it. "The time of justice has now come," he said, "and no force can hold it back."

Unofficially, King was said to have been so moved that his eyes were red and brimming with tears as he watched the speech. Officially, he said Johnson "revealed great and amazing understanding of the depth of the problem of racial injustice." Other civil rights leaders expressed similar sentiments.

C. T. Vivian called it "a victory like none other," adding, "It was an affirmation of the movement. It guaranteed us as much as anything could that we would vote and that millions of people in the South would have a chance to be involved in their own destiny."

John Lewis, who typically was distrustful of the president's political machinations, felt Johnson on this night "was a man who spoke from his heart, a statesman, a poet."

But James Bevel put it best, contending that it was actually more sermon than political speech. "I think there was a genuine sense of love and respect that went from Johnson to all people," he said. "The President wasn't politicking. He was very serious about what he was saying, and people heard him and they knew that he was right."[12]

But old suspicions die hard and old fears are not easily overcome. Some black observers were afraid that the speech was so strong it effectively made Johnson the nation's leading civil rights advocate. That made one, J. L. Chestnut Jr., uncomfortable. "It suddenly dawned on me that King was no longer the number one civil rights leader in America," he said. "Lyndon Johnson was. I was afraid we had been outfoxed and were in danger of being co-opted. If he .... set our agenda, did this mean the end of the movement?"[13]

Johnson's speech had a different but equally forceful effect on white segregationists. For the first time, many sensed the hopelessness of their cause. It all went downhill from there, Mayor Smitherman said. He called the speech a "dagger in your heart."[14]

******

On Thursday, March 17, Judge Frank Johnson heard the SCLC's petition for the right to march to Montgomery with police protection. Determined to be fair, Johnson thoroughly challenged both parties to the dispute at length. Following the hearing, he legally authorized the march.

Johnson's ruling set precedent by applying the traditional legal principle of proportionality to constitutional injury. As he explained the case, "It seems basic to our constitutional principles that the extent of the right to assemble, demonstrate and march peaceably along the highways and streets in an orderly manner should be commensurate with the enormity of the wrongs that are being protested and petitioned against. In this case, the wrongs are enormous."

Johnson ordered Wallace and the state of Alabama not to harass or threaten the marchers, even going so far as ordering them to provide protection from hostile whites. Although widely anticipated, Johnson's ruling was a major victory for King and his colleagues.

That Friday, an increasingly agitated Wallace telephoned President Johnson. Without actually saying it, he seemed to be pressing the president to intervene to have the march canceled or delayed. "We were hoping you could at least use your influence to make them have an orderly march," he said.

He told the president that his state troopers were so tied up in march control preparations that they were ignoring their typical highway duties. Meanwhile, he said, people were "pouring in" from all over the country, "priests and nuns and hundreds of bearded beatniks."

Johnson appeared to enjoy Wallace's discomfort. "Well, governor, the court has spoken now," he drawled. "The longer the march is postponed now, the more problems you're gonna have and the more problems I'm gonna have and the more problems the country is gonna have. I think your concern is justified. You can get your troopers back to the highways and call up [the Alabama National Guard.] Maybe we'd have to federalize them. I would be glad to take those steps if you felt the orderly needs of the situation there justified it and required it. We just got to work together the best we can. I'm willing to do this, if that's what you want."

Wallace quickly discarded that suggestion. "I don't want to be in the position of intimating that I'm asking for federal troops," he said.

Johnson pressed harder: "I think it would be better for you to call up the Guard. And if the situation deteriorated, I would have to give some thought to federalizing the Guard. But we're confronted with a fact and not a theory, and if your patrolmen are going back to the highways and you got this group that's comin', if you called up the Guard, I'll put the best people we've got here to work right with 'em."

The conversation continued in this vein for about five more minutes, Johnson not-so-subtly pushing Wallace to ask for federal help and Wallace awkwardly fending off the idea.

Wallace said his Guard was on alert and would be called on if necessary. "We're gonna take whatever measures needed to protect the marchers, but we can't guarantee that nobody's gonna get hit with a rock or something."

Johnson countered again that immediate Guard action was preferable. "Call up your Guard," he said flatly. "We'll have people available and alerted if you don't have enough."

Wallace finally appeared to relent, telling Johnson: "I'm just as concerned as you are about nothing happening. If it takes 10,000 Guardsmen, we'll have them. I'll just do whatever's necessary."[15]

But the next night, Wallace went on statewide television and denounced the ruling from Judge Johnson's "mock court." He also double-crossed the president, proclaiming that Alabama did not have the resources needed to ensure the safety of the marchers. Essentially decoupling himself from the issue, Wallace said that Johnson would have to act if he wanted to provide adequate protection. It was not so much a request as it was an ultimatum. After having told the president earlier in the day that he would do "whatever's necessary," Wallace was now in effect saying it wasn't his problem. He called on Johnson to provide sufficient federal "civil" authorities for the "safety and welfare of the so-called demonstrators."

Upon hearing reports of the telecast, President Johnson called Wallace "a no-good son of a bitch." The president then issued a statement, turning the "states' rights" argument around to use against Wallace:

> *"Responsibility for maintaining law and order in our federal system properly rests with the state and local government. On the basis of your public statements and your discussions with me I thought that you felt strongly about this and indicated you would take all necessary actions in this regard. I was surprised, therefore, when in your telegram on Thursday you requested federal assistance in the performance of such fundamental duties. Even more*

surprising was your telegram of yesterday, stating that both you and the Alabama legislature, because of monetary considerations, believed that the state is unable to protect American citizens and to maintain peace and order in a responsible manner without federal forces."[16]

Time for diplomacy had run out. Johnson signed an order federalizing the Alabama National Guard units and a second document ordering Secretary of Defense Robert McNamara to dispatch sufficient regular U.S. Army troops to ensure the marchers' protection. Despite all the arm-twisting and political maneuvering, Johnson got the only concession he really needed. The president did not have to unilaterally order federal troops into action; they were being mobilized only because Wallace said the state could not afford them. They were not hostile intruders forcing their way in; they were there only because Wallace had chosen to abdicate the state's responsibilities. That distinction was critical to Johnson, who didn't want to be perceived as having unleashed an invading force on a sovereign state.[17]

It was now just four days before the scheduled march to Montgomery.

Chapter 15: Walking to Montgomery

While the SCLC's legal team was feverishly preparing for the injunction hearing, the group's planners had been hashing out the logistical details required to move thousands of people on foot along a busy state highway for 54 miles.

Judge Johnson actually cut the organizers a break when he ruled that only 300 people could march once the highway narrowed to two lanes outside of Selma, giving the entire group a span of about 7 miles to cover at the start and another 10 miles or so when the highway widened to four lanes again west of Montgomery. That restriction, to which King readily agreed, eased the logistical burden considerably. Still, march rules had to be established and arrangements had to be made for food and sleeping accommodations.

King was anxious that the march be construed as one of "good will" that was sanctioned both legally and constitutionally. He insisted that marchers not walk on the actual highway or tie up traffic in any other way and was relieved when Hosea Williams reported that it would be possible to walk single-file across the three bridges on the route.

The group would need several spots along the walk to pitch tents. For those not willing to camp out, vehicles were required to provide morning and evening shuttle services. Security was needed, of course. And what would be done with all the trash that was certain to accumulate?

It was a tough, detail-oriented planning process, and though the cause was noble, the work was tedious. Said Young, "There was absolutely nothing romantic about it."[1]

Tents were rented, and more than 50 support vehicles – ambulances, latrine trucks, a water truck, a mobile clinic and more – were rounded up on loan and made ready for action. Women from black churches in Selma and Montgomery baked bread and cooked fish, ham, chicken, potatoes and a variety of other dishes. Huge pots of soup were prepared.[2]

A scan of records from that week illustrates the scope of the task:

700 air mattresses at $1.49 each

700 blankets donated by local churches and schools

Four carnival-size tents rented for $430 apiece

700 rain ponchos

Two 2,500-watt generators

2,000 feet of electrical wiring

The list went on ...[3]

Meanwhile, the typically sleepy Montgomery airport was teeming with activity that stretched its resources to the maximum and beyond. People arrived steadily throughout the week in numbers the airport had never seen before. They came from all regions of the country and were as remarkable for their diversity as their numbers.

Factory workers, college professors, firemen, school teachers, businessmen, housewives and many others were there.

Representing a broad cross-section of American people, they were white and black, young and old, wealthy and poor.

The airport quickly ran out of rental cars, leading march organizers to establish a car pool shuttle system to get their supporters to Selma.

******

Sunday, March 21, dawned bright and windy in the Black Belt. Selma was pulsating with excitement and activity. Huge jets were landing at nearby Craig Air Force Base, transporting some 2,000 U.S. Army soldiers and all their gear. Officers were transported to the Selma National Guard Armory and a telephone hotline was established with the Pentagon. Helicopters whirred overhead.[4]

Downtown Selma was jammed with marchers, onlookers and assorted political and religious dignitaries who had arrived for the occasion. But the heart of the gathering was the huge throng of everyday people. Most of these folks had no personal stake in the struggle but felt so strongly about the cause that they were willing – indeed, eager – to travel hundreds of miles or more to participate in an event that involved personal sacrifices and posed very real safety concerns.

The *Selma Times-Journal* reported: "Priests, nuns, ministers and rabbis walked. Beatnik types were there. So were white women, civil rights leaders, a Negro pushing his baby in a stroller. Some were well-dressed, some wore Levi's."[5]

By President Johnson's order, they would be guarded by the 2,000 soldiers, 1,800 national guardsmen, 100 FBI agents and 100 federal marshalls. Helicopters and light planes would watch from above.

The announced departure time for the march was 10 a.m., but organizers were once again running late. King and

Abernathy finally arrived at about 1 p.m. "Walk together, children," King shouted. "Don't you get weary and it will lead us to the promised land."[6]

March director Hosea Williams beamed as some 3,500 marchers stepped off for the first leg of the procession, a 7-mile march to the beginning of two-lane highway, where most would have to turn back due to safety concerns, as per Judge Johnson's ruling.

As the procession slowly unfolded, the marchers began singing "We shall overcome." Curious whites standing along the curbsides observed the proceedings. Most were silent, but several shouted racial epithets and others held racist placards.

Among the marchers were Nobel Peace Prize winner Dr. Ralph Bunche, a United Nations undersecretary, and a one-legged white man from Michigan, who hobbled along on crutches. Cager Lee, Jimmie Lee Jackson's 82-year-old grandfather, managed to keep pace for a few miles, declaring, "Just got to tramp some more," before yielding to the aches and pains of old age.

Selma Mayor Smitherman said he was glad the marchers were gone but afraid they might return. The rest of Selma's white community held its collective breath, grateful for the respite but concerned, like Smitherman, that it might only be temporary.

Marion, meanwhile, seemed like a ghost town, with many of its black residents either in Selma or on the road to Montgomery.

******

Most of the reporting for the following day-by-day accounts of the historic march was provided by the *Selma Times-Journal.* Although editorially, the paper was unapologetically segregationist, its news reports were, for the most part, fair and thorough. Race beat reporters from across the country discovered they could rely on the *Times-Journal* for accuracy and detail, something that could not be said of many of the other small-town papers they encountered across the South.

The *Times-Journal's* march coverage was both balanced and insightful. Reading carefully, one can detect a tone that at times seems almost sympathetic.

Sunday -- The marchers covered about 8 miles on Sunday, ending the day by pitching their tents in a farm field along the highway. National Guardsmen kept round-the-clock watch over the camp. Patrols rotated on guard duty, retiring at intervals to their pup tents for some sleep.

Monday -- Day 2 began with a breakfast of oatmeal, toast, jelly and coffee as the 300 or so chilly marchers broke camp in the frost-covered farm field at about 8 a.m. The temperature had dipped below freezing Sunday night, but Monday dawned clear and crisp, with steadily rising temperatures.

As the marchers approached one service station Monday, the white operator closed the station and placed a wooden barricade across the driveway.

Marchers had to contend with racial slurs shouted by passing motorists, but most seemed more troubled by painful foot blisters. Among those turning out to watch the march was Lowndes County Sheriff Frank Ryals, who expressed disdain for the event, "This march is uncalled for," he said. "It's a lot of expense for nothing."

At the time, Lowndes County had exactly one registered black voter in a county where blacks outnumbered whites 4-1. In the 10 years he had been sheriff, Ryals said, the county had not experienced any similar upheavals.

The throng covered 17 miles Monday and was almost to the halfway point before stopping to set up camp in a pasture near the Big Swamp of Lowndes County owned by Rose Steele, a black store owner.

Like every day of the march, the threat of violence was always present and the marchers were wary every time an automobile carrying hostile whites would pass. They were also subject to the stares of the white farmers who would come out to watch the march mostly in silence.

But victory was in sight, and the tension was balanced by the excitement the marchers felt.

T**uesday** -- Spirits clouded along with the weather Tuesday morning as the marchers set out in a light but steady rain. As the column departed the field, a woman marcher fainted and was taken away by ambulance. Other marchers bickered over the rigid march rules and were admonished by Bevel to quit complaining and obey orders from the marshalls.

At this point, the march had almost become anti-climactic. The spirited sense of adventure that sent the marchers on their way Sunday had succumbed to the less exciting realities of sore feet, soaked clothes, fitful sleep and inadequate facilities. After three uneventful days, public attention was also shifting from Alabama to Washington D.C., where President Johnson was aggressively promoting his voting rights bill.

Still, by the end of the day, marchers had closed to within 14 miles of Montgomery. They spent the night on a soggy hill near Lowndesboro. The sleeping area was covered with fresh-cut hay, but the rest of the site was a muddy quagmire

Wednesday – The final leg of the 50-mile march began at about 7 a.m. Wednesday, an hour earlier than usual. Marchers were greeted by a warm spring sun, which was a welcome sight after Tuesday's dreary, all-day rain.

The goal for the day was to get inside Montgomery city limits and make camp in the yard of a Roman Catholic school some 6 miles from the Alabama Capitol.

Meanwhile, the stage was being set for what was sure to be an eventful final day. Abernathy told newsmen the march was "the greatest demonstration for freedom in the nation since Abraham Lincoln signed the Emancipation Proclamation." Young said that chartered trains and planes would bring people to Montgomery for the Capitol stretch from New York, Washington, Los Angeles, Chicago and other major cities.

In Montgomery, meanwhile, Police Commissioner L. B. Sullivan asked citizens to stay away from Thursday's demonstrations at the Capitol.

Thursday – Montgomery, the old capital of the confederacy, looked like an occupied military zone on Thursday. Hundreds of Alabama National Guardsmen under federal command and Army regulars, rifles slung over their shoulders, patrolled Dexter Avenue leading to the state Capitol. Army helicopters circled the scene, as did two military planes.

Despite Police Commissioner Sullivan's appeal, the march route was lined with excited spectators, both black and white.[7]

******

Fearing for King's safety, Andrew Young secretly implemented a security plan designed to confuse any would-be snipers. Knowing that many black preachers, like King, preferred blue suits, and banking on the commonly held belief that most whites think blacks all look alike, Young summoned some 15 blue suit-clad ministers to march with King at the head of the procession, pushing a handful of unhappy celebrities and other well-known hangers-on to less prominent positions.

The marchers thus triumphantly entered Montgomery led by 15 ministers, all dressed alike, flanking King. Said Young: "They never did find out why they were there. But they loved it."[8]

Roy Reed of the *New York Times* described the entrance to the city as "grandeur that was almost Biblical." Said Reed: "The little band that made the entire march, much of it through desolate lowlands, was joined by thousands who flocked to Montgomery to walk the last three and a-half miles of the trek to the Capitol." He estimated the crowd at 25,000; others put it much higher.[9]

King's speech in front of the state Capitol was an emotional high point and fitting conclusion to the five-day march. He began with an anecdote about an elderly black woman he called "Sister Pollard," who was an active supporter of the Montgomery bus boycott some 10 years earlier. "One day," King said, "she was asked while walking if she didn't want to ride. And when she answered, 'No,' the person said, 'Well, aren't you tired?' With her ungrammatical profundity, she said, 'My feets is tired, but my soul is rested.'"

And now, King added, "We can say that our feet are tired, but our souls are rested."

King said the movement would not be deterred. His voice choked with emotion, he proclaimed, "Today I want to tell the city of Selma, today I want to say to the state of Alabama, today I want to say to the people of America and the nations of the world, that we are not about to turn around. We are on the move now. Yes, we are on the move and no wave of racism can stop us. ... The burning of our churches will not deter us. The bombing of our homes will not dissuade us.... The beating and killing of our clergymen and young people will not divert us."

The crowd unleashed a huge roar that would have been easily audible some 100 yards away in the office of Gov. Wallace, who was seen several times parting the blinds of an office window overlooking the rally.

Having established the movement's determination, King directed his thoughts to the future. He implored his followers to remain committed to the nonviolent approach, saying, "Our aim must never be to defeat or humiliate the white man, but to win his friendship and understanding. We must come to see that the end we seek is a society at peace with itself, a society that can live with its conscience."

Acknowledging that many blacks were growing impatient and asking "How long will it take," King had a succinct response: "Not long."

His voice rising as he neared his conclusion, King proclaimed, "I come to say to you this afternoon, however difficult the moment, however frustrating the hour, it will *not be long,* because "truth crushed to earth will rise again."[10]

But the buoyancy of the moment was tempered by the reality of the times. As the exuberant Montgomery crowd dispersed and many marchers headed for the nearest restroom, an "out of order" sign quickly went up at a nearby gas station.[11]

Reflecting on the march in his autobiography, edited by Clayborne Carson, King waxed poetic:

> *"The thousands of pilgrims had marched across a route traveled by Sherman a hundred years before, but in contrast to a trail of destruction and bloodshed, they watered the red Alabama clay with tears of joy and love overflowing, even for those who taunted and jeered along the sidelines. Not a shot was fired. Not a stone displaced. Not a window broken. Not a person abused or insulted. This was a triumphant entry into the 'Cradle of the Confederacy.' And an*

entry destined to put an end to that racist oligarchy once and for all."[12]

The Selma movement was essentially over, but the violence was not. As SCLC leaders and volunteers celebrated the successful march that night and countless visitors scrambled to make arrangements to get home, word came of another senseless death.

Viola Liuzzo a 39-year-old white Detroit housewife, was brutally murdered Thursday night as she drove along a dark and lonely Highway 80 with a young black man. Liuzzo, the wife of a Teamsters Union local official and the mother of five children, had asked her husband for permission to help in Selma. Fearing for her safety, he agreed with the proviso that she would not march or demonstrate.

Assisting in the "transportation section," Liuzzo's role at the conclusion of the march was to pick up marchers in Montgomery and ferry them back home to Selma. Each round trip on Highway 80 was 108 miles, and every volunteer driver was expected to make two trips.

Liuzzo and her passenger, 19-year-old Leroy Moton, were returning to Montgomery for more passengers after taking one group back to Selma after the march. Moton was assigned as a guide to Liuzzo's car.

About 30 miles out of Montgomery, Liuzzo noticed a car following her and Moton. Concerned but not alarmed, she kept a wary eye on the car, repeatedly checking her rearview mirror. Several times the car sped up close behind Liuzzo, only to fall back. Just after Liuzzo crossed the Big Swamp Creek in rural Lowndes County, the car pulled up again but instead of pulling back this time, it veered into the other lane and pulled up alongside Liuzzo's vehicle. Several shots were fired, shattering the driver's side window. Liuzzo was killed by a bullet to the temple. The car careened off the road and traveled several hundred yards into a pasture, finally coming to a stop against an old barbed-wire fence. Moton, who was unharmed, saw a car approaching from the other direction and played dead, crumpled on the floor of the car, lying perfectly still. He heard footsteps and excited voices, and then someone aimed a flashlight beam at the front seat. The next thing he heard was retreating footsteps, a car door slam and the car roaring off into the night.

It was the third violent death of the Selma/Marion movement and clearly illustrated the magnitude of the task that lay ahead. When they should have been celebrating their greatest achievement to date, movement leaders were instead mourning the loss of another life. Two of those who had died were white, one was black. None of the three were protest leaders, just everyday people who had heeded the call to help others in distress.

Less than 24 hours after the shooting, the FBI announced that it had arrested four white men for the murder of Liuzzo. Although it was never publicly acknowledged, one of the men, 31-year-old Gary Thomas Rowe of Birmingham, was working as a paid secret FBI informant at the time. After the shooting, Rowe alerted his FBI contacts, who then swooped in the next day to make the arrests.

Worried that he and the FBI might be blamed in part for the murder, an anxious J. Edgar Hoover called President Johnson early the next morning, Friday, March 26, seeking to preemptively distance the agency from any claims of complicity or inadequate protection of civil rights workers. It was still about five hours before the arrests would actually be made. The following conversation ensued:

Hoover: (We had) one of our men in the car. Fortunately, he, of course, had no gun and did no shooting. But he has identified the two men who had guns and who fired guns. I think there were 10 or 12 shots fired into the car.

Johnson: Six-shooter or shotgun?

Hoover: I think they're revolvers. They discussed that after it was over, if the woman died, they were going to throw the guns into the blast furnace where they worked in those steel mills down there. That's what we're laying for now, to head off those individuals when they come to work this morning and shake them down …

Johnson: What is an infiltrator and an informant? You hire someone and they join the Klan?

Hoover: No, we go to someone who is in the Klan and persuade them to work for the government. We pay him for it. Sometimes they demand a pretty high price … For instance, in those three bodies they found in Mississippi [August, 1964] we had to pay thirty thousand dollars for that. Now this man that we have now, this informant, he's not a regular agent of the Bureau. But he's one of these people that we put in, just like we do into the Communist Party, so they'll keep us informed. And fortunately, he happened to be in on this thing last night. Otherwise, we would be looking for a needle in a haystack.

Johnson: That's wonderful, Edgar. Thank you so much.[13]

At 12:40 p.m. Friday, a grim President Johnson, flanked by Hoover and Katzenbach, went on television to announce that four Klansmen had been arrested for Liuzzo's murder. He didn't reveal that one of the suspects was, in fact, an FBI informant.

Johnson said: "Mrs. Liuzzo, who went to Alabama to serve the struggle for peace, was murdered by the enemies of justice who for decades have used the rope and the gun and tar and feathers to terrorize their neighbors." He described the Klan as a "hooded society of bigots."

The three Klansmen charged with Liuzzo's murder were found not guilty by an all-white Alabama jury, but later served six years each on a federal conviction for violating Liuzzo's civil rights.

The actual shooter, Collie LeRoy Wilkins, a Birmingham resident, was tried twice in Alabama courts in 1965. During the first trial his lawyer stressed that Rowe was violating a Klan secrecy oath by testifying. Ten members of the jury supported a manslaughter conviction, but the other two held out, saying they could not believe a man who violated his oath. The judge declared a mistrial.[14]

The second trial was even easier for Wilkins. It was essentially over before it began as the Alabama Supreme Court refused to allow the prosecution to exclude white supremacists and Citizens' Council members from the jury. Wilkins was found not guilty and quickly became a celebrity at Klan parades and rallies.

Abernathy and other black civil rights leaders were outraged because everyone knew these men were guilty and should have been convicted of first-degree murder. "We had forgotten the way justice operated in south Alabama in those years," he said years later. "Despite the fact that an eyewitness had testified for the prosecution, for a while it appeared the murderers would go completely free." In fact, Abernathy said, the absence of proper punishment for Liuzzo's killers embittered many movement operatives, pushing them toward a more violent agenda.[15]

Rowe entered the federal witness protection program. At a 1975 Senate hearing, he said he had beaten Freedom Riders, killed a black man and sowed dissent within the Klan by sleeping with Klansmen's wives, all with the encouragement of the FBI.

By the time the Selma-Montgomery march took place, the initial goal of the Selma campaign – the introduction of federal voting rights legislation -- had already been achieved, but that didn't mean the march was without purpose or in any way redundant. As historian Adam Fairclough notes in his book *To Redeem the Soul of America,* the march gave southern blacks compelling evidence that their efforts had the full support of the federal government. And on an emotional level, the march symbolized the defeat of die-hard segregationists, a source of pride and confidence for the black community.[16]

Chapter 16: Congress Gets Busy

Lyndon Johnson didn't waste any time following up on his We Shall Overcome speech. In fact, the lobbying began before he had even left the House floor.

As an emotionally drained but still-focused Johnson walked slowly down the center aisle of the raucous chamber, he was pressed on all sides by excited well-wishers, many of whom were former colleagues. Among those greeting Johnson was Emanuel Celler, chairman of the House Judiciary Committee.

"Manny," Johnson said, leaning in so Celler could hear him above the noise. "I want you to start hearings this week." Stunned, Celler managed to stammer that he had scheduled hearings for three days the following week. But Johnson persisted: "Start them *this* week, Manny. And hold night sessions, too."[1]

Understanding the ephemeral nature of public opinion, Johnson wanted to move *now*, before segregationist forces could slow his momentum. He was optimistic but determined to leave nothing to chance.

Sen. Richard Russell of Georgia, one of Johnson's closest personal friends, had led the fight against the Civil Rights

Act of 1964 but health problems would prevent him from doing so this time around, putting southern lawmakers at a significant disadvantage. Though an outspoken and unapologetic segregationist, Russell commanded the respect of his colleagues, Democrat and Republican, liberal and conservative. He was a dignified and reserved man who knew as well as anyone how to use Senate parliamentary rules and procedures to his advantage.

Russell believed in white supremacy but like Lyndon Johnson early in his political career, he showed no animosity or hatred for blacks, and denounced white politicians who sought to exploit racial fears for political gain. Though their views on race had diverged over the years, Johnson still considered Russell a close friend and mentor.

But where he once was a formidable presence, Russell's influence had diminished considerably in recent years, due to both ill health – he suffered from pulmonary edema – and a series of votes that placed him outside the political mainstream on many major issues, including federal aid to higher education, the nuclear test-ban treaty, and the War on Poverty legislation. Even healthy, Russell likely would not have been able to significantly alter debate over an extremely popular bill.[2]

The most senior southerner after Russell was Allen Ellender, a 75-year-old senator from Louisiana. Ellender, too, was respected for his intelligence and integrity, and was a logical choice to lead the fight against the voting rights bill. Despite his game attempts, however, it became clear early on that the southerners no longer had the strength or numbers to effectively resist the inexorable push toward a strong voting rights act.

As a liberal senator told the Saturday Evening Post in March: "The southern generals are still brilliant, but their troops are old and tired, and there simply aren't enough to go around."[3]

That there would be a voting rights bill was a foregone conclusion. The only remaining questions were: When? And, how far would it go?

******

The Voting Rights Act of 1965, as submitted to Congress on March 18, was not an isolated, self-contained piece of legislation, but it did introduce some interesting new concepts to the American body politic. It evolved slowly yet logically from previous efforts to address black voter registration problems, including the civil rights acts of 1957, 1960 and 1964. In essence, the intent of the act was simply to provide a means for enforcing the Fifteenth Amendment, which had been law for 100 years.

The Fifteenth Amendment, passed in February 1869, is often considered as significant for what it left out as for what it said. The amendment was short and vague. Simply, it prohibited denial of the vote based on "race, color, or previous condition of servitude."

While well-intentioned, it gave southern politicians plenty of room to devise not-so-subtle ways of keeping blacks out of the voting booth. As noted earlier, the Fifteenth Amendment and subsequent court orders clearly supported the *principle* of voting rights for all but were also riddled with loopholes through which white political leaders could effectively delay or deter the registration of black Americans.

It had become clear that broad, general statements, on this issue at least, would not be enough. Detailed legislation that painstakingly delineated process and enforcement was also necessary. In that context, legislation to ensure minority voting rights would not signal a philosophical shift or provoke a constitutional crisis, it would merely seek to clarify and enhance that which already existed. Unlike the women's suffrage movement of the 1920s, which was aimed at getting women the right to vote, black Americans already had that right. The problem was that it was being arbitrarily denied by southern officials seeking to defeat the spirit of the law by subjecting it to their own creative interpretations.

Katzenbach's bill addressed that problem through a three-pronged approach:

1. Abolish literacy tests

In drafting the new bill, Katzenbach and his Justice Department colleagues were determined to eliminate any registration hurdles that could be used to suppress the black vote, which meant drafting language codifying the federal suspension of literacy tests. And while that now seems fairly benign, in 1964, it provoked a great deal of internal hand-wringing.

In 1959, the U.S. Supreme Court had given its blessing to fairly administered literacy tests. The Court held that "the ability to read and write ... has some relation to standards designed to promote intelligent use of the ballot." But acknowledging the likelihood of mischief, the court also said that "a literacy test, fair on its face, may be employed to perpetuate that discrimination which the Fifteenth Amendment was designed to support."

When working toward the Civil Rights Act of 1964, therefore, the Kennedy Administration proposed a bill to ban the "unfair" use of literacy tests, but noted that the measure did not prevent states from requiring that voters be literate and capable of reason.

Thus, when proposing a federal ban of literacy tests, the Johnson administration chose to argue not whether literacy should be a prerequisite for voting, but whether the tests were being administered fairly, which, a wealth of evidence illustrated, they were not. And despite the 1959 Supreme Court ruling, Attorney General Katzenbach argued that Congress had the power to prohibit any practices used to deny rights guaranteed by the 15th Amendment.

This approach made some members of the administration uncomfortable. One argued that the ban "might place the President in the indefensible position of advocating 'illiteracy' as a qualification, rather than a disqualification for voters," and another worried about "the incompatibility of an illiterate minority with the successful functioning of our Democratic system."

But Katzenbach knew that any literacy test – whether deemed fair or unfair – could be manipulated to the satisfaction of the registrar. He had a powerful argument prepared for those who would rather standardize the tests than abolish them: "Discrimination in education rendered literacy tests inherently unfair even if fairly applied."[4]

Using a trigger mechanism to establish uniform voting standards in the most recalcitrant states, the administration's bill called for the abolishment of literacy tests in states and jurisdictions where less than half the voting-age citizens had voted in or registered for the 1964 general election.

The new law also sought to ban the practice of requiring would-be voters to have an already-registered voter provide a positive character reference before they could register. With no Supreme Court ruling to the contrary and a long list of "voucher" abuses on the record, officials were confident they could abolish this practice without judicial interference.

2. Require pre-approval of changes

Katzenbach inverted another long-standing legal dictum in proposing that the law require covered states to seek federal government approval of any voting-practice changes before making them. To do so, the state would have to convince the attorney general or the District of Columbia's District Court that the change would not result in racial discrimination.

This provision differed from the normal legal process in which the attorney general would have to prove a state was discriminating in order to get relief. To insist on the reverse – the state having to prove that it was *not* discriminating – was unprecedented.

Still, the pre-clearance component was considered essential in that it would not only prevent a state from regressing but also ensure that local governments would not be able to delay equal voting rights through endless legal appeals.[5]

3. Deploy federal examiners

The Voting Rights Act of 1965 relied on administrative, rather than judicial, enforcement. Federal "examiners" would be inserted to oversee the registration and election process. Appearing before Congress, Katzenbach argued that the current litigation approach had not worked, noting that for legislation to be successful, it was necessary for it to be administered fairly by state officials, which was problematic in the Deep South.

The examiner provision differed from earlier efforts to use federal "referees" in several significant ways:

- The examiners would be appointed administratively rather than judicially.
- Examiners didn't have to reside in the locale of registration.
- Prospective voters need not apply to the board of registrars before applying to the examiner.

Using the same 50 percent turnout trigger, six states would immediately qualify for federal examiners: Mississippi, South Carolina, Alabama, Virginia, Georgia, and Louisiana. Also qualifying would be 34 counties in North Carolina and one county each in Arizona and Maine.[6]

Left unaddressed was the thorny issue of poll taxes.

******

On March 18, Senate Majority Leader Mike Mansfield asked the Senate to refer the voting rights bill to the Senate Judiciary Committee with instructions to report it by April 9. That didn't set well with committee chairman James Eastland of Mississippi, who said, "Let me make myself clear. I am opposed to every word and every line in the bill." Later that day, the Senate voted to give Eastland's committee a 15-day deadline. Even with the chairman's strident opposition, there was little doubt the measure would be reported favorably.

Eastland's Senate committee and Emanuel Celler's House Judiciary Committee both approved bills that were actually stronger than the administration's version, with the Senate panel adding a ban on poll taxes in local and state elections. But Johnson worried that the poll tax ban, while ostensibly strengthening the bill, was rife with legal pitfalls and could actually hurt the black registration cause. In 1937 and 1951, the Supreme Court had rejected the sentiment that poll taxes were de facto violations of the Fifteenth Amendment. And as Katzenbach told Johnson: "Should the court hold the ban unconstitutional, thousands of first-time voters in Alabama, Mississippi and Virginia, who had been misled into failing to pay their taxes, may lose their vote in important state elections."

Katzenbach also pointed to the dangerous possibility of "the very seriously damaging impact of a judicial declaration of unconstitutionality with respect to any portion of the Voting Rights Act of 1965."

Despite the administration's concerns, prominent Senate liberals, including Massachusetts freshman Edward Kennedy, believed that an outright ban was both constitutional and desireable. But Senate Minority Leader Everett Dirksen, who was adamantly opposed to a ban, refused to budge, setting up a serious confrontation over the legislation.

For the first time since introducing his legislation, Johnson entered the debate, telling the Senate that he personally favored a ban but didn't want to jeopardize the entire bill by including a provision that was constitutionally questionable.

On April 30, Dirksen and Mansfield offered a substitute for the Senate Judiciary Committee bill that finessed the poll tax issue. In place of an outright ban, the substitute bill authorized the attorney general to initiate court proceedings against any poll taxes being used to discriminate.

On May 11, the Senate rejected Kennedy's amendment to abolish the poll tax by a vote of 45-49, but the provision was still alive in the House. One day later, Celler's House Judiciary Committee approved a voting bill that included a poll tax ban.

The road seemed clear to final Senate approval, but desperate southern senators weren't done yet. Introducing dozen of amendments and insisting that each be thoroughly debated, they tried gamely to slow down the voting bill juggernaut, but it was a futile exercise. On May 25, the Senate imposed cloture, thus ending the southern filibuster, by a vote of 70-30.

With the filibuster over, southern opposition collapsed. Senator Sam Ervin of North Carolina said, "The way things are, I don't think I could get a denunciation of the crucifixion in the bill." The next day, the Senate voted 77-19 to send its version of the voting rights bill to the House.[7]

On July 9 the House approved the voting rights bill – including the poll tax ban – by a margin of 333-85.

House and Senate conferees were confident they could reconcile the two versions of the bill, since the only significant difference between the two was the poll tax issue. However, an odd alliance of House liberals and House Republicans were firm in their support for the poll tax, albeit for different reasons. The liberals didn't believe the Mansfield/Dirksen Amendment went far enough, while Republicans were hoping the poll tax provision would bring down the entire bill, as Johnson feared.

King and Johnson discussed the poll tax issue during a lengthy telephone conversation that began at 8:05 p.m. on July 7, one day before the House approved the voting rights bill. This conversation between Johnson and King was the first time a ranking House liberal or prominent civil rights leader had signaled that they truly understood what was at stake. Heretofore critical of the Senate bill because of its "weaker" poll tax provision, movement leaders and their liberal supporters were now beginning to understand what Johnson had been saying all along: a poll tax disagreement risked killing the entire bill.

At the time, Johnson was miffed over public comments King had made recently in opposition to the Vietnam War, as well as the civil rights leader's apparent mistrust of his handling of the voting bill, and the July 7 conversation lacked the usual introductory small talk, beginning instead with this frosty exchange:

King: Hello

Johnson: Yes?

King: Yes, President Johnson?

Johnson: Yes.

King: This is Martin King.

Johnson: Yes?

King: How do you do, sir?

Johnson: Fine.

King: Fine. I'm glad to hear your voice.

Johnson: Thank you.

Unsure of the strategy the administration was using in regard to the poll tax, King and his colleagues had been insisting on an outright ban, but after an earlier conversation with Katzenbach, King now realized what was at stake, telling Johnson, "It would stand in the way of everything we've tried to get in the voting bill."

Johnson tried hard not to say "I told you so," but couldn't help admonishing King and his colleagues during a lengthy monologue: "We are confronted with the realistic problem of the South and the Republicans. I think the civil rights leadership is coming around now to see the problem that we all have. If they don't have much confidence in the attorney general, they're going to be in trouble anyway because he's the man we have to rely on to help us."

He then engaged in some presidential self-pity for having to carry this message alone:

"There's been nobody really around here shoving it. I've done the best I could, but they're hitting me on different sides, and the press is kind of … Vietnam or the Dominican Republic or some mistake here or some mistake there. I'm getting cut up a little bit. [Roy] Wilkins [president of the NAACP] is having a national convention, and you were somewhere else. I called George Meany [AFL-CIO president] to ask him to help, but he'd gone to Europe. I called [Walter] Reuther [head of the UAW], but he won't be back until August … We are all off celebrating and doing something else, and they're going to put a package together that I can see forming."

King tried to speak, but Johnson was rolling and wouldn't be stopped:

"Now the smart thing to do – if we had people that would all stay with us and follow leadership – would be to get some language that the [Congressional] Leadership Conference would agree on. Go in and see McCormack and our friends and say, now, let's take this language that the Senate will accept without it going to conference so we can go on and get this bill passed and start registering our people. That's what we need to do. They're playing us and we're not parliamentary smart enough."

And:

"If you want to be honest now, I'm just telling you. You all are either going to have confidence in me and in Katzenbach, or you ought to pick some leader you do have and inform him. Now, I started out on this voting bill last November right after the election. I called them down and told them what I was going to do. I called you down here and told you what I was going to do. I went before Congress and made a speech and asked them to work every weekend. Then we all went off, and they haven't had any heat except from me. They're getting tired of the heat from me."

King and Johnson proceeded to discuss the future of the bill and as the conversation was winding down, King told the President his earlier remarks on Vietnam had been taken out of context, saying, "I know the terrible burden and awesome responsibilities and decisions that you have to make are very complicated and didn't want to add to the burdens because I know they're very difficult."

Johnson told King he appreciated his thoughts and then launched another 10-minute explanation about the difficulties of his job and the frustrations of being misunderstood and unappreciated.[8]

Three weeks later, with House and Senate conferees still wrangling over the poll tax, King told Katzenbach that the Senate's poll tax provision, if vigorously pursued, would be an effective vehicle "to finally bury this iniquitous device." The next day, brandishing King's statement, Katzenbach finally persuaded House liberals to yield to the Senate on poll tax language.

The final piece was in place. House members passed the conference report 328-74 on August 3. The following day the Senate followed suit by a margin of 79-18.

Two days later, on August 6, Johnson went to the Capitol to sign the Voting Rights Act of 1965. Before signing the bill, he called it "one of the most monumental laws in the entire history of American freedom."[9]

******

Johnson's signature on the Voting Rights Act of 1965 was the most significant achievement of the civil rights movement to date. Importantly, it was much more than symbolic and offered much more than hope. Freed from the onerous literacy tests and now dealing with federal examiners instead of racist county registrars, blacks began registering in record numbers across the Deep South.

The administration didn't wait long to begin enforcing the law. Within just a few months, more than 100,000 blacks were registered in Alabama, Louisiana, Mississippi, and South Carolina. Also, a key Supreme Court decision in 1966 eliminated any use of the poll tax, as the administration had anticipated.

Over the next 20 years, black voter registration rates in Alabama went from 19.3 percent to 68.4 percent. In Mississippi, they went from 6.7 percent to 69.9 percent.

Numbers for several other key southern states were: Georgia, 27.4 percent to 56.8 percent; Louisiana, 31.6 percent to 77.1 percent; North Carolina, 46.8 percent to 58.2 percent; South Carolina, 37.3 percent to 56.7 percent; and Virginia, from 38.3 percent to 63.8 percent.

Those states also saw a significant increase in the number of elected black officials at the local and state levels.

But while the rousing victory of the Selma campaign marked an emotional and operational peak for the civil rights movement, it also signaled the beginning of the end. The Watts riots, which erupted in Los Angeles on August 11, just five days after Johnson signed the Voting Rights Act, served as a call-to-arms for black America, and King's devotion to nonviolence suddenly seemed outdated and naïve.

The riots, which began in the Watts neighborhood when a white police officer arrested a black motorist, resulted in 34 deaths, more than a thousand injuries and some $40 million in property damage. Moreover, it sent a message to the rest of America that the quest for equality was rapidly evolving into a violent campaign for black power.

The civil rights movement, which began with the Brown v. Board of Education ruling on school desegregation in 1955, had effectively pressed the black case for equal rights through nonviolent protest and orderly legislative process, but time – and patience -- had run out.

The SCLC soldiered on through an ill-fated northern campaign based in Chicago, and King remained the most prominent voice for civil rights until his death in April 1968, but other voices – louder and more strident – were beginning to resonate in the nation's black communities.

Stokely Carmichael, who replaced Gandhian disciple John Lewis as the head of SNCC in 1966, gave his first "Black Power" speech after being arrested during a Mississippi march less than one month after taking over at SNCC. Upon his release, he proclaimed, "We been saying 'Freedom' for six years. What we are going to start saying now is 'Black Power!'" [10]

Carmichael used the phrase to promote black pride and socioeconomic independence, saying: "It is a call for black people in this country to unite, to recognize their heritage, to build a sense of community. It is a call for black people to define their own goals, to lead their own organizations."

Lewis's dedication to King's nonviolence philosophy was directly responsible for his downfall as SNCC chairman. The election of Carmichael illustrated nothing so much as the widening gap between the movement's King/Lewis faction and the increasingly impatient SNCC field workers.

Said Carmichael: "The SNCC people had seen raw terror and they understood properly this raw terror had nothing to do with morality but had to do clearly with power. It was clear that [Lewis] had been alienated from the SNCC staff ... His policies were not capable of holding up with the direction SNCC had to go."[11]

From there, it was just a short journey to "Burn Baby Burn" and the violent riots that wracked so many American cities later in the decade.

Like Carmichael, many Black Power adherents supported the notion of black autonomy, a direct rebuke of King's vision of peaceful integration.

King advisor Bayard Rustin, one of the SCLC's co-founders, was a harsh critic of the burgeoning Black Power movement. In 1966, Rustin wrote that Black Power "not only lacks any real value for the civil rights movement, but ... is positively harmful. It diverts the movement from a meaningful debate over strategy and tactics, it isolates the Negro community, and it encourages the growth of anti-Negro forces."

Rustin was particularly harsh on CORE and SNCC for embracing Black Power. He argued that these two organizations once "awakened the country, but now they emerge isolated and demoralized, shouting a slogan that may afford a momentary satisfaction but that is calculated to destroy them and their movement."

The fragile civil rights coalition had been shattered.

Looking back, John Lewis would say that Selma and the voting rights campaign had kept the movement together despite increasing internal friction. "After that," he said, "we just came apart."[12]

Urban rioting and cries of "Black power" toppled the movement from its perch on the moral high ground, alienating many previously supportive Americans and greatly complicating King's mission.

Split by dissension and uncertain how to proceed, the SCLC moved north to tackle poverty in big-city ghettos, but by 1966 the national political climate had changed beyond recognition. George Wallace rode a wave of white backlash to national prominence, and a reinvigorated alliance of conservative southern Democrats and northern Republicans successfully fought further reform efforts.

As author Adam Fairclough so aptly put it, "With bewildering suddenness, the SCLC stood isolated and impotent, bereft of political influence. Confused, divided and weary from battle fatigue, the black movement in the South ground to a halt. Within a year, it had virtually disintegrated."

Chapter 17: James Bonard Fowler

Alabama District Attorney Michael W. Jackson was just slightly more than one year old when Jimmie Lee Jackson was killed. Nearly 50 years later, he would play the lead role in bringing Jackson's assailant to justice, thus closing the book on one of the civil rights movement's most significant events, one that had been obscured by the darkness of night and the mists of time, and remained dormant through the turn of the century despite the attention being given to other 1960s-era "cold cases."

District Attorney Jackson (no relation to the victim) was born in tiny Fayetteville, Tennessee, just north of the Georgia state line, on Nov. 18, 1963. He graduated from the Florida State University College of Law in 1988 after getting his undergraduate degree from Centre College in Danville, Kentucky.

In 2004, Jackson was elected the first black district attorney in Alabama's fourth judicial circuit, a five-county area that includes Selma and Marion. He first gained national recognition for his role in working out a plea arrangement with three Birmingham college students accused of burning down nine churches in rural Alabama in 2006. Four of those churches were located in Bibbs County, part of Jackson's judicial circuit, and had black congregations. The three students were white.

Most of the time, however, his workday is spent on more typical community problems. Jackson's office handles more than 4,000 cases a year, the majority of which are drug-related crimes, often involving gangs, theft, and gun-related incidents.

Like most Alabama residents of a certain age, Jackson was aware of the 1965 shooting of Jimmie Lee Jackson, but his grasp of the details had diminished with time. So little had been said or written about the case in so many years that he and many others assumed that the state trooper who pulled the trigger – publicly identified only as "Fowler" -- had died. Regardless, Jackson and his small staff of assistants had plenty of cases to keep them busy, including the church burnings, and weren't inclined to go looking for more.

But after being out of the headlines for so many years, an account of the shooting resurfaced in a March 6, 2005, article in the *Anniston Star*, a daily newspaper located about 150 miles northeast of Selma. And for the first time, the shooter was identified by his full name – James Bonard Fowler. Written by editor-at-large John Fleming, the lengthy article was a remarkably thorough recounting of events surrounding Jimmie Lee Jackson's death, but Fleming's real coup was obtaining an interview with Fowler, the first time the retired trooper had spoken publicly since the shooting.

Fowler, then 70, agreed to the interview with Fleming because he wanted to tell his side of the story. He believed he was immune from prosecution. Not only had a previous grand jury declined to hand up an indictment back in 1965, the passage of time had blunted whatever fears he once had.

"I don't think legally I could get convicted for murder now no matter how much politics they got 'cause after 40 years they ain't no telling how many people is dead," Fowler said.

Throughout the interview, Fowler speaks in a folksy, matter-of-fact manner. He could just as easily be discussing the weekend weather or the Monday night football game as his role in a historic shooting death.

In comments that closely tracked his sworn statement 40 years earlier, Fowler said he was merely acting in self-defense. Showing no remorse and expressing no regret, he told Fleming, "Jimmie Lee Jackson was not murdered. He was trying to kill me and I have no doubt in my mind that under the emotional situation at the time, that if he would have gotten complete control of my pistol that he would have killed me or shot me. That's why my conscience is clear."[1]

Before the 2005 interview, Fowler had never even been publicly identified as the trooper who shot Jackson. Thanks to the racist attitudes of the times and the benevolent support of Gov. George Wallace and State Patrol Commander Al Lingo, Fowler immediately returned to work after the shooting until leaving of his own accord in 1968.

When a grand jury declined to indict him in September 1965, prosecutors also declined to reveal his identity, save the mention of his surname: Fowler.

But by publicly acknowledging that he had, in fact, pulled the trigger, Fowler unwittingly generated interest in a long-dormant case. And for the first time, the shooter not only had a name, he had a face.

Journalist Fleming was reluctant to discuss the interview when contacted eight years later but did say this about Fowler: "He is an extremely intelligent man and that's what made him interesting. He's not some ignorant redneck."

Soon after the article appeared, District Attorney Jackson began hearing from people encouraging him to re-open an investigation into the shooting death of Jimmie Lee Jackson. People would call to offer their support. People he ran into on the street or encountered at social functions would pull him aside to tell him something should be done.

While other mishandled civil rights-era cases were re-opened and aggressively prosecuted, the Jimmie Lee Jackson file had remained closed. The people in Marion hadn't forgotten, but most other state residents, including those in major media markets, had moved on. Meanwhile:

- In 1994, Byron De La Beckwith, a white supremacist and Klansman from Greenwood, Mississippi, was convicted of assassinating civil rights leader Medgar Evers outside Evers' home in Jackson on June 12, 1963. Two previous trials in 1964 had resulted in hung juries.
- In 2002, four men were convicted in a 1963 bombing that killed four young girls at the 16th Street Baptist Church in Birmingham, Alabama.
- On June 21, 2005, a Mississippi jury convicted Edgar Ray Killen on three counts of manslaughter for the 1965 deaths of civil rights workers Michael Schwerner, Andrew Goodman and James Chaney. Killen, then 80 years old, was sentenced to three consecutive terms of 20 years in prison.

Jackson was intrigued by the notion of re-opening the Jimmie Lee Jackson case but skeptical that much could be done given the passage of 40 years. He quietly began to research the case, reviewing old newspaper clippings and tattered, yellowing police reports. "Anything I could find, I dug up," he said. And the more he dug up, the more interested he became.

Taking the next step, Jackson drove 30 miles up Highway 14 from Selma to Marion, where he visited the scene of the alleged crime and interviewed local residents for their recollections of the incident. He looked primarily for older residents who might have been around 40 years earlier, and found plenty of them willing to talk. "They started telling me about things that happened during that time, about what was going on," Jackson said. Unfortunately, none of them were eyewitnesses to the shooting.

Returning to his cluttered office on the third floor of the Dallas County Courthouse, just three blocks from the Edmund Pettus Bridge, Jackson reviewed the reports with a small group of assistant D.A.s, and weighed the merits of his case. At best, he determined, it was a long shot, but he felt obligated to try.

Jackson says he didn't feel any pressure to pursue charges against Fowler, but thought it was the right thing to do given the importance of the Voting Rights Act and also "to give closure to Jimmie Lee Jackson and history." He and his staff continued to gather evidence, but the trail was cold and progress was slow. At issue was not whether Fowler had actually shot Jackson – he readily admitted that – but whether he was acting in self defense.

Jackson believed it was an unlawful killing, but needed more evidence before taking the case to a grand jury. "We need one final piece," he told his team.

That final piece came in the form of a statement from Vera Booker Jenkins, a former night nurse supervisor at Good Samaritan Hospital in Selma, where Jimmie Lee Jackson had been taken after the shooting. Jenkins told District Attorney

Jackson she was on duty the night Jackson was shot and talked to him briefly while he was awaiting treatment. She claims Jackson told her he didn't know why he had been shot, he was just trying to protect his family.

Based on the evidence his office had gathered, and the nurse's statement, Jackson decided it was time to proceed. A racially mixed grand jury was seated in Perry County on May 8, 2007, and returned a sealed indictment after hearing two hours of testimony.

During the hearing, several witnesses corroborated Jimmie Lee Jackson's version of events as told to the hospital nurse. District Attorney Jackson also introduced photographs of Jimmie Lee's mother and grandfather, beaten and bruised.

One day later, James Bonard Fowler appeared in court to hear the charges against him. He was indicted on one count of first degree homicide (intentional) and one count of second degree homicide (unintentional) for the shooting of Jimmie Lee Jackson, more than 40 years earlier. The action, in effect, reversed the decision of two grand jury investigations, one state and one federal, that dismissed the case in 1965, claiming there wasn't enough evidence to indict Fowler.

District Attorney Jackson was pleased with the indictment, and said it was possible only because the cultural milieu had changed so much since 1965. "It just never would have been a really thorough investigation (back then)," he said following the grand jury's decision. "Things were a lot different back in the '60s."

But Fowler's defense lawyer, high-profile Birmingham attorney George Beck, maintained that his client was innocent and cautioned against a rush to judgment. "I think that we have to be real careful in discriminating between those acts of intentional violence as opposed to the trooper who's trying to protect the public, who may be trying to act on orders of his supervisor," Beck said. "And I don't think that every civil rights injury and killing means that something was done illegally."[2]

At the time, Beck was considered one of the best defense attorneys in Alabama, an indication that Fowler was taking the charges seriously. "A lot of these people (civil rights cold case defendants) hired old Klan attorneys, but Fowler didn't," journalist Fleming said. "He knew what he was doing."

Regardless, the indictment of Fowler didn't really come as a surprise. As one observer put it, "You could get a grand jury to indict a ham sandwich."

With the indictment in hand, it was time to prepare for trial. The circuit judge assigned to the case was lifelong Selma resident Tommy Jones. Tanned, fit and energetic, Jones looked more like a golf pro than a circuit court judge in his early 50s, but in fact was a highly respected jurist.

On November 8, 2007, Jones presided over the arraignment and then held hearings on several key issues, including the 40-year delay between incident and indictment. The defense asked for the case to be dismissed, arguing that the inordinate amount of time that had elapsed would make it impossible for Fowler to get a fair trial. Beck noted that many people who would have testified, including Sheriff Clark and Governor Wallace, had since passed away. Beck also insisted that the *cause* of Jackson's death was critical to his defense. Several doctors at the time claimed that Jackson did not die from gunshots wounds, but rather from an infection caused by a bungled surgery. Those doctors, Beck said, were no longer available to testify.

District Attorney Jackson countered that the lengthy delay had hurt the prosecution far more than the defense. "The state has the burden of proving this case beyond a reasonable doubt," he said. "We are the ones that have to put this case together." Like the defense, he said, the prosecution had also lost several potential witnesses.

Jackson also scoffed at the notion that Fowler's gunshot was not responsible for Jimmie Lee Jackson's death. "We have to go back to what the standard of care was for blacks in 1965," he said. "The reason he was in the hospital is because he got shot by Mr. Fowler. To say that he didn't receive good treatment doesn't alleviate the problem that he was shot and killed by Mr. Fowler."

Beck sought to buttress his case for dismissal by eliciting testimony from Coleman C. Keane, a retired FBI special agent currently living in Chattanooga, Tennessee. Keane said he was assigned by FBI Director Hoover to gather domestic intelligence on events in Selma and Marion, and personally observed the Marion violence.

His observations sounded like they came directly from Hoover's playbook. He said the state troopers that night were "organized, well-disciplined, supervised properly and led properly." He also claimed to have seen black demonstrators throwing rocks and bricks, which he believed they had stockpiled behind the church.

In his official report of the incident, Keane called the shooting of Jimmie Lee Jackson a "clean shoot," by which he meant there was "no untoward responsibility on the part of the officer." Keane said he didn't see any troopers snatching cameras from reporters or television crews, and insisted that police did nothing to provoke the violence.

The testimony was damaging to the state's case, and on aggressive cross examination, Jackson attempted to portray

Keane as a product of the segregated South, someone whose observations likely had been tainted by his personal biases.

Keane contended that he could clearly see everything that happened that night, but Jackson got him to acknowledge that the scene was blanketed in darkness.

Jackson: "Are you aware that pretty much all accounts say that it was dark out there at the time all of this was going on?"

Keane: "It was dark, yeah."[3]

Years later, the district attorney described Keane, who had inserted himself into the proceedings by contacting Fowler's defense team after reading a newspaper account of the indictment, as a crackpot. "They were coming out of the woodwork," he said of the old segregationists. "Right out of left field."

While saying he still hoped for dismissal, Fowler's attorney also implemented a backup plan. Beck asked for a change in venue, contending that it would be impossible for his client to get a fair trial in a county that considered Jimmie Lee Jackson a martyr in the fight for civil rights, going so far as to rename a highway in his honor.

Judge Jones took the defense requests under advisement, eventually ruling against dismissal and holding the change of venue request in abeyance until prospective jurors could be questioned in the *voir dire* process.

To say that the case was proceeding slowly would be more than a mild understatement. The next significant pre-trial hearing was held on September 19, 2008, nearly a full year after the initial hearing. Each side blamed the other for the lengthy delay, with both insinuating that political factors were at work. The defense believed Jackson was stretching out the proceedings for maximum publicity, while Jackson charged that the defense had caused the delay by waiting to see if he would be re-elected that July, which he was.

On June 3, 2008, Jackson was returned to office by a wide margin, easily winning all of his five counties. The Fowler trial was immediately reset and placed back on the docket.

"If I hadn't gotten re-elected ... that case would have been lost in the sunset," Jackson said. "So they waited to see if I was re-elected. It was clear as a bell." Jones, however, insists that Jackson's re-election prospects had nothing to do with the delays. He contends that Jackson had it within his power to expedite the proceedings, but chose instead to delay matters by filing his various motions and appeals at the last minute.

Following hearings on a number of other issues, most of them procedural, both sides were finally preparing to go to trial. Some 500 notices went out to potential jurors, a pool large enough to ensure that those ultimately chosen would be unbiased. "We wanted to make sure folks could be fair," Jackson said.

But just as the trial appeared ready to move forward, Judge Jones dropped a bombshell, ordering the prosecution to turn over its entire witness list, along with a summary of the anticipated testimony. The ruling was in response to a brief filed by Beck contending that the defense had no way of knowing if the grand jury indictment was based on actual legal evidence or was merely an emotional response to an incident that had shattered the community some 40 years earlier

At the September 19, 2008, hearing, Jones told both Jackson and Beck, "What I'm going to do, I'm going to order that the state provide to the defense counsel a list of all witnesses that the state intends to call involved in this case together with a short summary of what they expect their evidence to be." Turning to Jackson, he added: "I know you are going to object, but I want to get my order on the table anyway. And in addition to that, provide to the defendant any written or recorded statements that those witnesses have given to law enforcement."[4]

Jackson, who had taken to calling Judge Jones "Fowler's guardian angel," was stunned. He vehemently argued that the ruling violated Alabama law, but Jones would not be deterred.

Jackson immediately announced his intent to appeal the ruling through a writ of mandamus, further delaying the proceedings. The Court of Appeals eventually ruled in the judge's favor, but Jackson, still confident in his position, appealed to the Alabama Supreme Court, which ruled unanimously for the prosecution on September 4, 2010, nearly a full year after Jackson had filed his appeal and two years since Fowler had been arraigned.

Writing for the state Supreme Court, Justice Lyn Stuart said Judge Jones exceeded his discretion by ordering "the production of information specifically prohibited from production by the Alabama Rules of Criminal Procedure."

Jackson's concern over sharing the requested information was that it could be used to frighten his witnesses. "If they had the addresses of all these old folks I was going to call, they could be intimidated, like the kind of things going on back in the 60s" he said. "I didn't want my eyewitnesses to get scared."

Even after an interregnum of some 40 years, the ghosts of 1965 hovered over the proceedings.

But Jones says he never intended to frighten any witnesses. He claims he had an obligation to ensure that the evidence about to be presented by the state was legally admissible given the private nature of the Grand Jury hearing, Jones also says that while the state Supreme Court might have found fault with his approach, it supported his intent. "They just said I should have gone about it differently," he said.

Meanwhile, Jackson's relationship with Jones grew increasingly strained. Jackson was convinced that Selma's white power structure, as embodied by Jones, was trying to derail the Fowler trial, and Jones appeared frustrated with what he perceived to be Jackson's prosecutorial overreach.

The two men presented a fascinating study in southern culture and politics, post-1965. Jackson, a black man with humble beginnings in the Tennessee foothills, was openly challenging Jones, a white man with deep roots in Selma's aristocracy.

Jones grew up in the Mabry-Jones mansion, the home of his great-great grandfather, Catesby Jones, during and after the Civil War. Catesby Jones was a Confederate naval hero, who was in charge of the Naval Foundry at Selma, but is best remembered for commanding the Merrimac on the second day of her engagement with the USS Monitor at Hampton Roads, Virginia.

The home, which has been extensively remodeled over the years, features Civil War-era artwork and artifacts, giving it a museum-like feel. Prominently displayed on a library wall are framed sketches of Robert E. Lee and Stonewall Jackson, and the shelves are lined with books about southern history.

The home remains in the Jones family, but is used mostly for large family gatherings and community social functions. Ironically, District Attorney Jackson lives directly across the street from the Mabry-Jones mansion.

Jones freely acknowledges his lineal connection to the Confederacy, but makes no apologies for it. Times have changed, he says, and while he remains proud of his heritage, he insists that it doesn't define him or his beliefs.

Meanwhile, the courtroom surprises weren't over yet. In response to Jackson's writ of mandamus protesting the judge's witness list ruling, a brief written for Judge Jones suggested that Jackson was pursuing the case for political reasons and that Fowler couldn't possibly get a fair trial.

Taken aback yet again, Jackson promptly demanded that the judge recuse himself over this biased assessment. Jones refused, contending that the content of the brief did not necessarily reflect his opinion, but was merely a summation of witness testimony taken from court transcripts. Beck supported the judge, saying there was no evidence that Jones had done anything other than support the rule of law.

In August 2010, Jackson filed a formal motion for recusal, delaying the trial yet again. The motion was filed under an Alabama judicial ethics canon state that a judge should disqualify himself from a proceeding in which his impartiality might be reasonably questioned.

In another outstanding motion, Jones had not yet ruled on the prosecution's intent to introduce evidence from Fowler's personnel file, including reports that he had shot and killed a black man a year after the Jackson shooting, this time during a traffic stop that escalated into physical confrontation.

By now, the proceedings were hopelessly bogged down. More than two years after the grand jury was seated, parties to the dispute were still pointing accusatory fingers at one another. It was not yet known where the trial would be held, and the role of the presiding judge was shrouded in uncertainty. Meanwhile, elderly witnesses for both sides were growing infirm, and everyone involved seemed to be looking for a way out.

But the wheels of justice turn slowly, and another year would pass before there was further movement in the case.

At a hearing on August 17, 2010, Jones set a trial date of November 19, despite not having heard from the state on Jackson's recusal motion. Some three and a half years after Fowler had been indicted, the trial finally was set to begin, but it still wasn't known where it would be held or who would be presiding.

To the relief of virtually everyone involved, those questions never had to be answered. On November 15, the day prospective juror interviews were scheduled to begin, Jackson and Beck struck a deal to settle the case. The settlement was very favorable to Fowler. The two murder counts were reduced to a single charge of manslaughter, and the defendant would be sentenced to minimal time in jail.

All along, the obstacle to a settlement had been Fowler's insistence that he not serve any jail time. Jackson was firm on his demand that at least some jail time had to be part of any agreement, but Fowler and his team were just as firm in opposition. The big break came when Fowler consented to serve time in jail. A deal was quickly struck whereby Fowler would plead guilty to manslaughter and 1) acknowledge responsibility for killing Jimmie Lee Jackson, 2) serve six months in jail and 3) apologize to the Jackson family. These were District Attorney Jackson's three prerequisites for settling the case, and although he had hoped for a lengthier sentence, he decided there was no point in further negotiations, especially given the uncertain nature of his case.

The long saga of the death of Jimmie Lee Jackson appeared to be nearing an end, but not everyone was happy. The district attorney was immediately beset by a barrage of criticism that he had been too easy on Fowler. Civil rights leaders and members of Jimmie Lee's family argued that the six-month jail sentence was far too lenient. They didn't understand how such a notorious offense could be dismissed so lightly.

It was, in fact, a bittersweet victory. The district attorney and Jackson family members did not get the murder conviction they sought, but Jackson hoped the jail time and an apology from Fowler would help close a painful chapter in U.S. history. "I didn't wrangle over it, trying to squeeze a hundred years out of some guy who was already 80," Jackson said. "I wanted to make sure he spent some time in jail for what he had done."

But the slain man's cousin, Julia Greene Cash, said, simply, "The sentence was unfair. It wasn't right."

District Attorney Jackson also said Fowler's half-hearted apology left a bitter taste with the family. Speaking without emotion, Fowler said he didn't mean to kill anyone. "I was coming over here to save lives. I didn't mean to take lives," he said. I wish I could redo it."

While speaking, however, he refused to look at Jackson's family members, choosing instead to keep his eyes trained on the judge. "They were standing right beside me, but he just wouldn't look back at them," the district attorney said. "Normally, a defendant would look at the family and say 'I'm sorry,' but he just wouldn't do it."

To be sure, District Attorney Jackson faced a dilemma most other civil rights "cold case" prosecutors didn't – the accused was an officer involved in law enforcement, not a lay person carrying out a premeditated act of racial violence. He had other factors to consider as well.

Jackson was worried that Fowler might die before the trial was over. He also worried about the possibility of a hung jury and the effect that might have on the racially polarized town of Marion. "It was better to get Fowler to plead guilty and acknowledge responsibility for unlawfully killing Jimmie Lee Jackson," the district attorney said.

Defense attorney Beck said Fowler agreed to plead guilty to the reduced charge because he was concerned he couldn't get a fair trial in Perry County and his health was poor. "He wants to put it behind him," he said at the time. "It puts to rest a long chapter of civil rights history here in Perry County."

Jackson says Fowler wasted no time putting the ordeal behind him, thanks to an assist from the Alabama legal system. Scheduled to serve six months in the Geneva County jail in southern Alabama, Fowler was released early due to his poor health. The release was granted in a casual arrangement without benefit of a formal court hearing.

Judge Jones, meanwhile, was defeated in his 2010 re-election bid. He currently is practicing law with a Selma firm whose managing partner served as the city's chief legal counsel during the 1965 voting rights campaign.

Fowler, for his part, isn't talking. During a brief telephone conversation in March 2013, he declined to comment, saying "I'm not going to get back into that." Prodded, Fowler said the lengthy legal proceedings and subsequent jail term wore him down, adding, "That cost me years of my life and thousands of dollars in attorney fees." Asked about his health, Fowler would say only that he is "feeble." He then politely ended the conversation, saying "You have a good day, sir."

Chapter 18: Selma and Marion 50 years on

By most accounts, Selma, Alabama, in 2013 looks much the same as it did some 50 years ago. The central city and certain residential neighborhoods might be a bit more dilapidated, and some newer retail developments are visible – including the strip malls and fast-food joints along the outer edges of the city -- but the quintessentially southern essence of the city remains intact.

Approaching town from the east on state Highway 80, the gently rolling hills and pleasant roadside greenery give way to an outcropping of commercial billboards, many old and faded. Several highway-side businesses display neon "Open" signs, but many more are shuttered and in various states of disrepair. A low-rent housing project is seen to the south and it too is in great need of repair.

The famous Edmund Pettus Bridge, with its arcing steel framework, looms directly ahead, spanning the Alabama River. Downtown Selma awaits on the other side, the first signs of which are the decaying backs of many old wood-frame buildings perched precariously on the steep, sloping river bank.

Driving over the bridge is like traveling back in time. The downtown buildings may be old and worn but many hint at the architectural charm of a bygone era. The historic St. James Hotel, one of the last grand, old riverfront hotels in the Southeast, rests a block north of Broad Street, its stately presence enhanced by the cobblestone courtyard that graces its entrance, and the Dallas County Courthouse, ground zero for the 1965 voting rights campaign, remains unchanged at the northwest corner of Lauderdale Street and Alabama Avenue.

The retail shops in downtown Selma are mostly locally owned mom-and-pop establishments such as small drug stores, thrift shops, discount jewelers, and five-and-dime stores. Hints of the past remain: a rusting old "pay scale" in front of the corner drug store and many chipped and faded advertising messages painted on the brick sidewalls of corner buildings. There are signs of life – a recently renovated theater, some trendy boutiques, and a few busy cafes -- but many storefronts are vacant and worn. The downtown area seems busier than it actually is because of the traffic on Highway 80, which becomes Broad Street, Selma's main street, on the west side of the bridge. From the east, Highway 80/Broad Street is the only way to enter the city.

Some of Selma's residential neighborhoods still boast stately antebellum mansions, many of which are considered state historical sites, and several that have been in the same family for generations. The carefully maintained homes, with their white colonnades and wrap-around porches, are vestiges of a distinct regional heritage, and the tidy, well-kept grounds bespeak pride of ownership. Towering hickory and moss-draped live oak trees provide a leafy green canopy for much of Selma, with a variety of colors and pleasant fragrances provided by a decidedly southern array of plants and flowers, including magnolias, rhododendrons, and azaleas. The air is thick with the sweet scent of lilac bushes. Once the exclusive province of a white city majority, these neighborhoods have become racially mixed with the growth of Selma's black middle class.

Impressive as they are, however, Selma's upscale residences are greatly outnumbered by the weathered clapboard shanties and decaying brick ranches found in many other parts of the city. In these mostly black sections of town, residents gaze out at patchy lawns with little or no landscaping. Pock-marked sidewalks and weed-strewn lots abound. The appearance is harsh, but residents there worry more about gang violence and corner drug deals than curbside appeal.

Safety in Selma, like most towns, is more an issue today than in years past. The city is plagued by crime, much of which is black on black. A white lifelong Selma resident nursing a beer at the Tally-Ho, an aging supper club tucked away in a poplar grove on the north side of the city, says Selma, like the Tally-Ho, used to be a fine place. "I live just four blocks from downtown," he said. "I used to walk down there and back all the time, even at night. Now I wouldn't let my dog walk downtown alone."

Distinct southern flourishes aside, the disparities visible in Selma's socioeconomic picture are no different than many other cities, regardless of geographical location, yet they somehow seem more pronounced. That, perhaps, is a function of the city's reputation for racial strife, past and, to a lesser degree, present.

Most residents seem to agree that race relations in Selma and nearby Marion circa 2014 are better than they were 50 years ago. However, that assessment invariably comes with a qualifier. Yes things have improved:

... *but* we still have a long way go to.

... *but* the improvements are mostly superficial.

... *but* blacks and whites still share a mutual distrust.

Selma Mayor George Evans, who is black, doesn't actually verbalize the qualifying "but," when asked about the current state of race relations in his city. He doesn't have to. "Well, they're better ..." he says, drifting into a silence that speaks volumes.

After a long pause, Evans adds, "We have a ways to go yet. We still haven't gotten there. But I can say that it's better, and I believe it will continue to get better."

Evans, a former city council president, was elected mayor in 2008 and re-elected in 2012. A lifelong Selma resident, he went off to college in Dodge City, Kansas, in 1964 and was away from home during the landmark events of 1965. Having left "two" cities behind – White Selma and Black Selma – Evans returned several years later to find a single Selma, though one still rife with racial discord.

Some city residents, he says, are unwilling or unable to put racial issues aside for the greater good. "There are still groups on both sides that create drama and want to make everything black and white," he says. "To me, it shouldn't be about black and white. It should be about what's right, and that's what I try to base my decisions on."

As mayor, Evans must contend every day with the realities of racial discord. For him, mistrust between white and black residents is not an abstract social phenomenon, but rather a fact of life that he must consider in virtually every decision he makes, whether something as minor as a low-level appointment or as critical as economic development, job growth, public education, and the provision of basic city services.

It's no small task, but Evans, a thoughtful man with a calm, easy-going manner, seems to have earned the trust of both blacks and whites. He insists that progress is being made, not just on matters of official city business but on the ephemeral issue of race relations. Initiatives aimed at fostering greater trust between the races have been helpful, including one in which blacks and whites meet at someone's home once a month for fellowship and informal conversation. "We talk about life, not politics," Evans says. "We talk about how we can make Selma a better place."

No one would deny the value of such programs, but nor does anyone dismiss the magnitude of the task.

In 1965, Selma was roughly evenly divided between white and black residents, but as of the 2010 U.S. Census, the city's population of 20,000 was about 80 percent black and 18 percent white. Median household income for the city is $23,457, and some 40 percent of the population lives beneath the poverty line.

Racial politics has been an undeniably significant aspect of Selma's social fabric since approval of the Voting Rights Act of 1965, which resulted in the massive registration of black voters and subsequent election of many black candidates. As noted earlier, the numbers of both have increased exponentially over the years. But while that in itself is significant, those successes have not translated to improved socioeconomic conditions for most black residents of Selma, the Black Belt, or most other predominantly black areas of the Deep South.

Many white residents of the city are frustrated that the black political leadership has been unable to significantly improve living conditions and build a stronger economy. Blacks counter that the political might they now enjoy is stunted because whites continue to wield most of the area's economic power. Publicly, both groups embrace the need to work together for the benefit of all. Privately, many chafe at the perceived failings of the other side.

Suspicions abound. Many whites believe that blacks in public office run their communities primarily to benefit themselves, while many blacks believe the area remains poor because of the white economic power structure's reluctance to invest in the black community.

Racial tension has been a polarizing force across Alabama for generations, and many experts believe the Black Belt has been its source. Sam Webb, a University of Alabama-Birmingham historian, called it a "constant obsession."

"Whites have felt under siege and blacks, who went through 150 years of being excluded, don't feel like they can trust whites to look out for their interests," he told the *Birmingham News* in a 2002 interview. "On both sides, you have this incredible suspicion where racial motivation is used to explain every situation."[1]

Former U.S. Rep. Artur Davis agrees, calling the Black Belt "one of the most racially polarized areas in the United States." Davis, a 1993 graduate of Harvard Law School, is a licensed attorney in Washington D.C. He represented Alabama's 7th Congressional District from 2003 to 2010, during which time he was named one of the 10 Best Congressmen in America by *Esquire Magazine*. An expert on race relations, Davis is widely admired for his keen intellect and rare ability to discuss matters of race objectively and dispassionately.

Davis notes that the Alabama Black Belt is actually racially integrated when it comes to such things as work, dining out, and shopping, but blacks and whites have very different social existences apart from those casual associations.

"Whites and blacks have very deep, ingrained notions of the other race," he said. "Each race remains fearful and suspicious of the other, and that's something that pervades and affects the politics and economics of the area."

Conversations with people of both races in Selma and Marion confirm Davis's analysis. Blacks, to a large degree, believe that whites are racists and that they control the money. They also believe there is massive discrimination in employment opportunities. For their part, whites believe that African-Americans tend to be corrupt, are not good workers and don't live the way they should.

Each side has a very strong suspicion of politicians of the opposite race.

"It's very difficult to overcome that," Davis said. "And that's something that continues to affect the region. There's a veneer of civility, a veneer of integration, but then underneath that veneer there are two communities that view each other in semi-hostile terms many years after the events of the 60s."

The struggle for true equality has been an emotional journey for many of the area's black residents. They acknowledge that progress has been made but worry that intractable racial divisions remain, divisions stemming from the roots of slavery and maintained by years of mutual mistrust, anger, and fear.

Nearly 50 years after their first public displays of discontent, the Marion foot soldiers suggest that race relations have improved, but they too are quick to add qualifying sentiments.

"It's somewhat better than it was back then," says Mattie Atkins.

Willie Nell Avery adds: "We need to work together more, and what I mean by that is, we support their programs but when it comes down to our programs, they refuse to support them."

John Ward echoes Davis's observations, saying difficult issues are often hidden beneath a thin layer of friendly cooperation. "On a general basis, just day to day, the relationship is fairly normal," he says. "But when it gets down to real issues where we all should be treated equal or given the same privileges, it will come down to the point where there is a difference."

Such intense racial polarization is due to several conditions endemic to the Black Belt. It starts with a large black political majority that has been in power for a number of years and extends to the fact that the white minority is not affluent, as is the case of downtown condo-dwellers in many urban areas, but is itself low-income. That demographic portrait – low-income communities on both sides, a black political base and a shrinking white economic base – creates feelings of resentment for all involved.

Davis believes that white flight contributes significantly to the problem. When whites abandon the area in large numbers, that makes it even tougher for those who remain behind because they become politically marginalized. "If the area were more racially divided it would probably be easier to build more coalitional politics," he said.

The feelings of resentment and mistrust manifest themselves most noticeably during local and state elections, which, while not surprising, serves only to exacerbate the already substantial racial divisions. Davis calls it the Politics of Mutual

Racial Recrimination, a paradigm created and perpetuated by abject poverty, a racially charged political history, and the racial demonizing that occurs during election campaigns.

In effect, each side has developed a political mythology that allows it to win elections within its own community while convincing its supporters that the other side is responsible for economic stagnation, poor schools, inadequate health care and a host of related social problems.

Even when two black candidates or two white candidates are pitted against each other in political contests, one becomes the white community's candidate and one becomes the black community's candidate.

But such racial posturing, which can be helpful in winning elections, clearly is not conducive to good governance. In fact, it plays a major role in keeping cities such as Selma from developing real solutions to the many problems they face.

Davis himself was a victim of high-stakes racial politics in his 2010 bid to become the first black elected governor in the Deep South.

Seeking to transcend the politics of mutual recrimination, Davis campaigned without the blessing of the state's black political leadership. He hoped to build a diverse coalition of voters in his campaign for governor, but was rejected by Democratic primary voters in favor of Ron Sparks, little-known state agriculture commissioner.[2]

Sparks, who is white, was endorsed by the state's four major black political groups, while Davis intentionally declined to seek their support, instead promising to bring change to Alabama politics by building a broad coalition of black and white voters.

Indeed, Davis sought to minimize race as a factor in the campaign and worked to show his independence from

President Obama. In a move that put him at odds with Democratic Party leadership, he opposed Obama's signature initiative, the Affordable Care Act health insurance law, more commonly known as Obamacare.

"I vigorously reject the insinuation that there is a uniquely 'black' way of understanding an issue, and I strongly suspect that most Alabamians will as well," Davis said in response to criticism of his position on Obamacare.[3]

But his strategy of creating a broad biracial base of voters in the primary race, well-intentioned though it might have been, fell considerably short. Davis had deliberately sought to circumvent the politics of mutual recrimination, but his vision was no match for the conventional racial wisdom of Alabama politics. Sparks defeated Davis by a double-digit margin.

Davis's experience lends credence to the theory that biracial coalitions of the contemporary South are in reality unstable alliances between two groups whose political views and objectives are fundamentally at odds; while blacks consistently favor government-sponsored social programs, whites of all classes increasingly see such programs as benefiting blacks at the expense of white taxpayers.

Many observers still wonder why adoption of the Voting Rights Act of some 50 years ago and subsequent shift of political power from white to black has not resulted in more and better opportunities for so many black residents still mired in poverty.

The quick answer, of course, is that change does not come easy, that problems dating back to the days of slavery, perpetuated by generations of mistreatment and addressed only at great personal sacrifice, are not easily or quickly resolved. That's accurate, as far as it goes, but it's merely an overview, a broad generalization that conveniently skirts the need for more critical analysis.

Some observers, black and white, believe that too many blacks saw the right to vote not as a means to an end, but as an end itself, thus failing to take full advantage of its possibilities. Selma Mayor Evans blames it on the law of unintended consequences. "We got the right to vote, but we relaxed, and that's what's sad about the whole thing," he says. "We took a lot of risks and lost some lives for the right to vote, but then we didn't take advantage of it like we should."

And while Evans doesn't minimize the extent to which racist attitudes continue to hamper the black community, he puts much of the blame on members of his own race. "I'm very disappointed in where we've come," he says. "We gained the right to vote, the right to be treated equally, and access to equal facilities, yet in gaining all that it looks like we lost our thirst and ability to do the right things."

Citing black crime statistics and academic performance rankings, Evans says blacks must take more responsibility for the current situation. Adults, he says, must be better role models, and parents must be more involved in the lives of their children.

He also believes people of both races should return to the ideals of the original civil rights movement. "A lot of people risked their lives and a lot of people lost their lives during that time," he says. "Sometimes things go on now where you wonder if people really appreciate the facts of what happened then. You wonder if we really have taken advantage of what was the *intent* of us all working together and getting along."

Another, related analysis suggests that black leaders expended so much energy obtaining the right to vote that they lacked the emotional wherewithal and physical stamina to take the next logical step, teaching citizens who had been disenfranchised for generations how to vote properly and preparing potential office-holders for the responsibilities of governing.

As a result, the rapid political realignment engendered by the Voting Rights Act gave way to crisis, not fulfillment, ushering in an era where many well-intended black residents were being elected to office without the background or training needed to govern effectively.

Author Fairclough calls it "the crisis of victory." He says, "White domination remained a political reality, white prejudice a persisting fact. And the civil rights movement had no program or plan for translating the notional equality of the law into the social actuality of shared wealth and power."[4]

That assessment was shared by no-less-an-authority than SCLC organizer James Bevel, who blamed movement leaders for failing to follow through on the voting initiative. Getting the vote wasn't enough, he said. People who had been disenfranchised for so long should have been shown how to responsibly handle that vote.

"When we didn't do that, we let the people down," he said. "When we didn't follow through, I think that injured people, and it injured the movement, and it lessened the dynamic and the potency of the democratic process."[5]

Racial tension is exacerbated by the area's nearly impossible economic challenge. With its agricultural industry in decline over the past 50 years, the Black Belt desperately needs new industry and outside investment, but racial discord and uncertainty over the area's political leadership are powerful deterrents to potential investors.

And for good or ill, the influence of race cannot be denied.

It is, says one prominent state legislator, "more powerful than money, than politics, than religion."

Afterword

Like many Black Belt residents, Alabama District Attorney Michael Jackson believes the shots that rang out at Mack's Cafe that February night in 1965 signaled the turning point of the entire civil rights movement. "It all started there," he said.

Over the years, the Selma march – which many Black Belt residents still believe should have been the *Marion* march – has been summarized in typical journalistic shorthand as a march in support of the right to vote, which it was. But what often gets neglected or minimized in these summaries is the spark that ignited the movement and led directly to the Selma march, that spark being a flash from the gun that killed Jimmie Lee Jackson.

No one knew it at the time, but echoes from that shot – and Jackson's subsequent death -- would reverberate through American society for generations.

Jackson's death inspired James Bevel to propose the Selma march, without which there would not have been any Bloody Sunday violence. And without the terrifying photos and newsreels from Bloody Sunday, the already flagging Selma campaign might not have been able to regain its momentum.

Lacking broad national interest, President Johnson likely would not have delivered his "We Shall Overcome" speech, and voting rights legislation would not have been put on the fast track. If and when such legislation was introduced, Congress, led by the powerful Southern voting bloc, doubtless would have been more deliberate and less accommodating.

That entire scenario is speculative, of course, as is any attempt to determine what kind of voting bill eventually would have emerged without the powerful impact of Bloody Sunday. Certainly a determined push was being made for such a bill even before the Jackson shooting, as evidenced by President Johnson's many comments to King. That leads some historians to suggest that Bloody Sunday might have given the act an unexpected jolt of momentum but didn't significantly advance its timeline. Author David Garrow, for one, notes that before the end of 1964, Johnson had decided to put forward voting rights legislation sometime during 1965. Garrow also notes that the basic contents of what would become the Voting Rights Act of 1965 had already been crafted onto a draft bill by March 5, two days before Bloody Sunday.[1]

However, other prominent historians note that Johnson already had a full legislative agenda pending – including many elements of his cherished Great Society program such as the Elementary and Secondary Education Act, Medicare and Medicaid, acts to protect water and air quality, an omnibus housing act and the creation of federal aid to the arts and humanities. Eric Goldman and Doris Kearns Goodwin have argued that those initiatives would have taken precedence over the Voting Rights Act had Bloody Sunday not occurred.

Also, a rapidly unraveling Vietnam War policy was consuming more of Johnson's time, leading Goldman, Kearns Goodwin, and others to believe that the Voting Rights Act might have been set aside for another day without the violence in Selma.

But such speculation, while interesting, is irrelevant. Bloody Sunday did in fact push voting rights to the fore regardless of the administration's original timeline. The consideration of alternative scenarios can lead to some fascinating debates, but ultimately is nothing more than historical guesswork.

What we do know is this: Two unlikely figures -- James Bonard Fowler, with his quick trigger finger, and Jimmie Lee Jackson, protective of his mother and grandfather – crossed paths at a critical moment in time. Because one is white and the other was black, their instinctive actions set in motion a chain of events that forever altered America's racial landscape.

The Selma Campaign End Notes

Chapter 1:

1. Branch, Taylor. *Pillar of Fire: America in the King Years, 1963-64* New York: Simon & Schuster, 1998, 516.
2. Nobelprize.org *The Official Website of the Nobel Prize*
3. Albert, Peter J., Hoffman, Ronald. *We Shall Overcome: Martin Luther King Jr. and the Black Freedom Struggle* New York: Da Capo Press, 1990, 25.
4. Wright, Kai. *African-American Archives: The History of the Black Experience Through Documents* Black Dog and Leventhal Publishers, Inc., 2001, 588
5. Garrow, David. *Protest at Selma.* New Haven and London. Yale University Press, 1978, 21.
6. Garrow, David. *Protest at Selma.* New Haven and London. Yale University Press, 1978, 2.
7. Branch, Taylor. *Pillar of Fire: America in the King Years, 1963-64* New York: Simon & Schuster, 1998, 523.
8. Halberstam, David. *The Children* New York: Random House, 1998, 482.
9. Young, Andrew. *An Easy Burden: The Civil Rights Movement and the Transformation of America* HarperCollins, 1996, 336.

Chapter 2:

1. Branch, Taylor. *Pillar of Fire: America in the King Years, 1963-64* New York: Simon & Schuster, 1998, 523.
2. White House telephone transcripts July 15, 1965.
3. Hampton, Henry; Fayer, Steve. *Voices of Freedom: An Oral History of the Civil Rights Movement from the 1950s through the 1980s* New York: Bantam Books, 1990, 210.
4. Carson, Clayborne. *We Shall Overcome: The Autobiography of Martin Luther King Jr.* New York: Warner Books, Inc. 1998.
5. Albert, Peter J., Hoffman, Ronald. *We Shall Overcome: Martin Luther King Jr. and the Black Freedom Struggle* New York: Da Capo Press, 1990, 62.
6. Chesnut, J.L., Cass, Julia. *Black in Selma: The Uncommon Life of J.L. Chestnut* New York: Farrar, Straus and Giroux, 1990.
7. PBS. *Eyes on the Prize: America's Civil Rights Movement,* 1986

Chapter 3:

1. Cobb, Charles Jr. *On the Road to Freedom: A Guided Tour of the Civil Rights Trail* Algonquin Books
2. Lesher, Stephan. *George Wallace: American Populist* Reading, PA.: Addison-Wesley; 1994, 376
3. Chesnut, J.L., Cass, Julia. *Black in Selma: The Uncommon Life of J.L. Chestnut* New York: Farrar, Straus and Giroux, 1990, 148.
4. Chesnut, J.L., Cass, Julia. *Black in Selma: The Uncommon Life of J.L. Chestnut* New York: Farrar, Straus and Giroux, 1990, 149.

5. Chesnut, J.L., Cass, Julia. *Black in Selma: The Uncommon Life of J.L. Chestnut* New York: Farrar, Straus and Giroux, 1990, 137.
6. Remarks at Trinity College SNCC Reunion, April 1988
7. Young, Andrew. *An Easy Burden: The Civil Rights Movement and the Transformation of America* HarperCollins, 1996, 341.
8. Fairclough, Adam. *To Redeem the Soul of America: The Southern Christian Leadership Council and Martin Luther King* p.211; Athens: University of Georgia Press, 1987.
9. Fairclough, Adam. *To Redeem the Soul of America: The Southern Christian Leadership Council and Martin Luther King* Athens: University of Georgia Press, 1987, 226
10. Lewis, John. *Walking with the Wind: A Memoir of the Movement* San Diego: Harcourt, Brace & Co.; 1998, 390
11. Hampton, Henry; Fayer, Steve. *Voices of Freedom: An Oral History of the Civil Rights Movement from the 1950s through the 1980s* New York: Bantam Books, 1990, 214.
12. Young, Andrew. *An Easy Burden: The Civil Rights Movement and the Transformation of America* HarperCollins, 1996, 299.
13. Young, Andrew. *An Easy Burden The Civil Rights Movement and the Transformation of America* HarperCollins, 1996.
14. Halberstam, David. *The Children* New York: Random House, 1998, 483
15. New York Times, Dec. 23, 2008

16. Lesher, Stephan. *George Wallace: American Populist* Reading, PA.: Addison-Wesley; 1994, 376
17. Carson, Clayborne. *The Autobiography of Martin Luther King Jr.* New York: Warner Books, Inc. 1998, 271.

Chapter 4

1. Fairclough, Adam. *To Redeem the Soul of America: The Southern Christian Leadership Council and Martin Luther King* Athens: University of Georgia Press, 1987
2. Fairclough, Adam. *To Redeem the Soul of America: The Southern Christian Leadership Council and Martin Luther King* Athens: University of Georgia Press, 1987, 226
3. Fairclough, Adam. *To Redeem the Soul of America: The Southern Christian Leadership Council and Martin Luther King* Athens: University of Georgia Press, 1987, 228
4. Hampton, Henry; Fayer, Steve. *Voices of Freedom: An Oral History of the Civil Rights Movement from the 1950s through the 1980s* New York: Bantam Books, 1990, 215.
5. Young, Andrew. *An Easy Burden: The Civil Rights Movement and the Transformation of America* HarperCollins, 1996, 335.
6. Chesnut, J.L., Cass, Julia. *Black in Selma: The Uncommon Life of J.L. Chestnut* New York: Farrar, Straus and Giroux, 1990, 175 ; New York: Farrar, Straus & Giroux.
7. Halberstam, David. *The Children* New York: Random House, 1998, 495

8. Chesnut, J.L., Cass, Julia. *Black in Selma: The Uncommon Life of J.L. Chestnut* New York: Farrar, Straus and Giroux, 1990, 185 ; New
9. Kotz, Nick. *Judgment Days: Lyndon Baines Johnson, Martin Luther King Jr. and the Laws that Changed America* New York and Boston: Houghton Mifflin, 2005
10. Branch, Taylor. "Pillar of Fire" *America in the King Years, 1963-64* New York: Simon & Schuster, 1998, 559.
11. Abernathy, Ralph David. *And the Walls Came Tumbling Down: An Autobiography* New York: Harper & Row 1989, 315
12. Chesnut, J.L., Cass, Julia. *Black in Selma: The Uncommon Life of J.L. Chestnut* New York: Farrar, Straus and Giroux, 1990, 175
13. Abernathy, Ralph David. *And the Walls Came Tumbling Down: An Autobiography* New York: Harper & Row 1989, 315
14. Chesnut, J.L., Cass, Julia. *Black in Selma: The Uncommon Life of J.L. Chestnut* New York: Farrar, Straus and Giroux, 1990, 195
15. Halberstam, David. *The Children* New York: Random House, 1998, 491.
16. Abernathy, Ralph David. *And the Walls Came Tumbling Down: An Autobiography* New York: Harper & Row 1989, 316
17. Remembering Selma pamphlet, Page 8
18. Hampton, Henry; Fayer, Steve. *Voices of Freedom: An Oral History of the Civil Rights Movement from the 1950s through the 1980s* New York: Bantam Books, 1990, 217.

19. Hampton, Henry; Fayer, Steve. *Voices of Freedom: An Oral History of the Civil Rights Movement from the 1950s through the 1980s* New York: Bantam Books, 1990.

Chapter 5

1. Abernathy, Ralph David. *And the Walls Came Tumbling Down: An Autobiography* New York: Harper & Row 1989, 317
2. Abernathy, Ralph David. *And the Walls Came Tumbling Down: An Autobiography* New York: Harper & Row 1989, 318
3. Abernathy, Ralph David. *And the Walls Came Tumbling Down: An Autobiography* New York: Harper & Row 1989, 304
4. Roberts, Gene; Klibanoff, Hank. *The Race Beat: The Press, the Civil Rights Struggle, and the Awakening of a Nation* New York: Vintage Books 2006, 382
5. Branch, Taylor. "Pillar of Fire" *America in the King Years, 1963-64* New York: Simon & Schuster, 1998, 564.
6. Garrow, David. *Bearing the Cross: Martin Luther King Jr. and the Southern Christian Leadership Council* . New York: William Morrow and Co., 1986, 381
7. Kotz, Nick. *Judgment Days: Lyndon Baines, Martin Luther King, and the Laws that Changed America* Houghton-Mifflin, 2005, 264
8. Kotz, Nick. *Judgment Days: Lyndon Baines, Martin Luther King, and the Laws that Changed America* Houghton-Mifflin, 2005, 270
9. PBS. *Eyes on the Prize: America's Civil Rights Movement,* 1986

10. Kotz, Nick. *Judgment Days: Lyndon Baines, Martin Luther King, and the Laws that Changed America* Houghton-Mifflin, 2005, 264-65

Chapter 6

1. Marable, Manning: *Malcolm X: A Life of Reinvention,* New York: Viking Press, 2011, 411
2. Lesher, Stephan. *George Wallace: American Populist* Reading, PA.: Addison-Wesley; 1994, 318
3. Hampton, Henry; Fayer, Steve. *Voices of Freedom: An Oral History of the Civil Rights Movement from the 1950s through the 1980s* New York: Bantam Books, 1990, 221-222.
4. Carson, Clayborne. *We Shall Overcome: The Autobiography of Martin Luther King Jr.* New York: Warner Books, Inc. 1998, 263.
5. Internal SNCC document
6. Kotz, Nick. *Judgment Days: Lyndon Baines Johnson, Martin Luther King Jr. and the Laws that Changed America* New York and Boston: Houghton Mifflin, 2005, 267
7. Kotz, Nick. *Judgment Days: Lyndon Baines Johnson, Martin Luther King Jr. and the Laws that Changed America* New York and Boston: Houghton Mifflin, 2005, 267-8
8. CRMVETS.org
9. Garrow, David. *Bearing the Cross: Martin Luther King Jr. and the Southern Christian Leadership Council* . New York: William Morrow and Co., 1986, 384
10. Garrow, David. *Bearing the Cross: Martin Luther King Jr. and the Southern Christian Leadership Council* . New York: William Morrow and Co., 1986, 390

11. Kotz, Nick. *Judgment Days: Lyndon Baines Johnson, Martin Luther King Jr. and the Laws that Changed America* New York and Boston: Houghton Mifflin, 2005, 269
12. Garrow, David. *Bearing the Cross: Martin Luther King Jr. and the Southern Christian Leadership Council .* New York: William Morrow and Co., 1986, 389
13. Lewis, John. *Walking with the Wind: A Memoir of the Movement* San Diego: Harcourt, Brace & Co.; 1998, 390
14. Roberts, Gene; Klibanoff, Hank. *The Race Beat: The Press, the Civil Rights Struggle, and the Awakening of a Nation* New York: Vintage Books 2006.
15. PBS. *Eyes on the Prize: America's Civil Rights Movement,* 1986
16. Hampton, Henry; Fayer, Steve. *Voices of Freedom: An Oral History of the Civil Rights Movement from the 1950s through the 1980s* New York: Bantam Books, 1990.
17. Young, Andrew. *An Easy Burden: The Civil Rights Movement and the Transformation of America* HarperCollins, 1996.
18. Lewis, John. *Walking with the Wind: A Memoir of the Movement* San Diego: Harcourt, Brace & Co.; 1998, 320
19. Abernathy, Ralph David. *And the Walls Came Tumbling Down: An Autobiography* New York: Harper & Row 1989

Chapter 7

1. Abernathy, Ralph David. *And the Walls Came Tumbling Down": An Autobiography* New York: Harper & Row 1989, 324

2. PBS. *Eyes on the Prize: America's Civil Rights Movement,* 1986
3. PBS. *Eyes on the Prize: America's Civil Rights Movement,* 1986
4. PBS. *Eyes on the Prize: America's Civil Rights Movement,* 1986
5. PBS. *Eyes on the Prize: America's Civil Rights Movement,* 1986
6. Selma Times-Journal, Feb. 18, 1965, P.1
7. New York Times, June 17, 2007
8. Clark, Jim. *I Saw Selma Raped: The Jim Clark Story* Selma Enterprises, Inc., 1966.
9. "Eyes on the Prize" television documentary; 1986
10. Levine, Bruce. *Fall of the House of Dixie: The Civil War and the Social Revolution that Transformed the South* New York: Random House, 2013, 9 6
11. Levine, Bruce. *Fall of the House of Dixie: The Civil War and the Social Revolution that Transformed the South* New York: Random House, 2013, 92-3
12. PBS. *Eyes on the Prize: America's Civil Rights Movement, 1986*
13. Marable, Manning: *Malcolm X: A Life of Reinvention,* New York: Viking Press, 2011, 458-9
14. Carson, Clayborne. *We Shall Overcome: The Autobiography of Martin Luther King Jr.* New York: Warner Books, Inc. 1998, 265
15. Garrow, David. *Bearing the Cross: Martin Luther King Jr. and the Southern Christian Leadership Council .* New York: William Morrow and Co., 1986, 393

Chapter 8

1. Landsberg, Brian. *Free at Last to Vote: The Alabama Origins of the 1965 Voting Rights Act* University of Kansas Press, 2007.
2. Young, Andrew. *An Easy Burden: The Civil Rights Movement and the Transformation of America* HarperCollins, 1996, 71.
3. "Remember Selma" souvenir history book; P. 8.
4. New York Times, April 15, 2000
5. Young, Andrew. *An Easy Burden: The Civil Rights Movement and the Transformation of America* HarperCollins, 1996, 352
6. Landsberg, Brian. *Free at Last to Vote: The Alabama Origins of the 1965 Voting Rights Act* University of Kansas Press, 2007, 115
7. Landsberg, Brian. *Free at Last to Vote: The Alabama Origins of the 1965 Voting Rights Act* University of Kansas Press, 2007, 130

Chapter 9

1. New York Times, Feb. 22, 2008
2. "Eyes on the Prize" television documentary.
3. Eyes on the Prize television documentary
4. Huffington Post, Petter Ognibene
5. FBI witness statement documents, Feb. 19, 1965.
6. Hampton, Henry; Fayer, Steve. *"Voices of Freedom" An Oral History of the Civil Rights Movement from the 1950s through the 1980s* New York: Bantam Books, 1990, 223
7. Hampton, Henry; Fayer, Steve. *Voices of Freedom: An Oral History of the Civil Rights Movement from the*

1950s through the 1980s New York: Bantam Books, 1990, 224.

8. Roberts, Gene; Klibanoff, Hank. *The Race Beat: The Press, the Civil Rights Struggle, and the Awakening of a Nation* New York: Vintage Books 2006

Chapter 10

1. Halberstam, David. *The Children* New York: Random House, 1998, 503.
2. New York Times, February 21, 1965
3. New York Times, Feb. 22, 1965
4. Jeff Moore, FBI witness statement
5. Charles Pryor, FBI witness statement
6. Jimmie Lee Jackson, FBI witness statement
7. Norma Reen Shaw, FBI witness statement
8. Dr. Arthur Wilkerson, FBI witness statement
9. Leeandrew Benson, FBI witness statement
10. Robert Tubbs, FBI witness statement
11. Hardis Jackson, FBI witness statement
12. LeeAndrew Benson, FBI witness statement
13. Selma Times-Journal, Feb. 21, 1965
14. State of Alabama Public Safety Report, File No. 51-23; Feb. 25, 1965
15. FBI files, John Doar memo of Feb. 27, 1965.
16. "Eyes on the Prize" documentary; interview Sept. 17, 1979
17. "Eyes on the Prize" documentary, interview Sept. 17, 1979
18. Halberstam, David. *The Children:* New York: Random House, 1998, 504.
19. Halberstam, David. *The Children:* New York: Random House, 1998, 504.

20. 2Eyes on the Prize television documentary
21. 2Roberts, Gene; Klibanoff, Hank. *The Race Beat: The Press, the Civil Rights Struggle, and the Awakening of a Nation* New York: Vintage Books 2006, 385

Chapter 11

1. New York Times, March 4, 1965
2. Lewis, John. *Walking with the Wind: A Memoir of the Movement* San Diego: Harcourt, Brace & Co.; 1998, 330
3. Lewis, John. *Walking with the Wind: A Memoir of the Movement* San Diego: Harcourt, Brace & Co.; 1998, 330
4. "Branch, Taylor *At Canaan's Edge: America in the King Years* New York: Simon & Schuster 1998, 4 0
5. "Eyes on the Prize" interview; Nov. 7, 1988
6. Greenhaw, Wayne *Fighting the Devil in Dixie,* Lawrence Hill Books, 175.
7. Abernathy, Ralph David. *And the Walls Came Tumbling Down: An Autobiography* New York: Harper & Row 1989, 326
8. New York Times; Nov. 17, 2000
9. Lewis, John. *Walking with the Wind: A Memoir of the Movement* San Diego: Harcourt, Brace & Co.; 1998, 336

Chapter 12

1. Lesher, Stephan. *George Wallace: American Populist* Reading, PA.: Addison-Wesley; 1994, 115
2. Chalmers, David. *Backfire: How the Ku Klux Klan Helped the Civil Rights Movement* Bowman and Littlefield, 2003, 2 3

3. Chalmers, David. *Backfire: How the Ku Klux Klan Helped the Civil Rights Movement* Bowman and Littlefield, 2003, 2 4
4. Lesher, Stephan. *George Wallace: American Populist* Reading, PA.: Addison-Wesley; 1994, 318
5. Lesher, Stephan. *George Wallace: American Populist* Reading, PA.: Addison-Wesley; 1994, 320
6. Lesher, Stephan. *George Wallace: American Populist* Reading, PA.: Addison-Wesley; 1994, 322
7. Lesher, Stephan. *George Wallace: American Populist* Reading, PA.: Addison-Wesley; 1994, 325
8. The Birmingham News, March 8, 1965
9. CRMVET. Org
10. Lewis, John. *Walking with the Wind: A Memoir of the Movement* San Diego: Harcourt, Brace & Co.; 1998, 339
11. Lewis, John. *Walking with the Wind: A Memoir of the Movement* San Diego: Harcourt, Brace & Co.; 1998, 340
12. Newsweek Magazine, March, 1965
13. New York Times, March 8, 1965
14. Internal SNCC document. Schomburg Center for Civil Rights
15. Lewis, John. *Walking with the Wind: A Memoir of the Movement* San Diego: Harcourt, Brace & Co.; 1998, 340
16. Lewis, John. *Walking with the Wind: A Memoir of the Movement* San Diego: Harcourt, Brace & Co.; 1998, 343
17. Selma Times-Journal, March 8, 1965
18. Lesher, Stephan. *George Wallace: American Populist* Reading, PA.: Addison-Wesley; 1994, 326

Chapter 13

1. Hampton, Henry; Fayer, Steve. *Voices of Freedom: An Oral History of the Civil Rights Movement from the 1950s through the 1980s* New York: Bantam Books, 1990, 229.
2. "Abernathy, Ralph David. *And the Walls Came Tumbling Down: An Autobiography* New York: Harper & Row 1989, 336
3. Abernathy, Ralph David. *And the Walls Came Tumbling Down: An Autobiography* New York: Harper & Row 1989, 338
4. Abernathy, Ralph David. *And the Walls Came Tumbling Down: An Autobiography* New York: Harper & Row 1989, 338
5. Abernathy, Ralph David. *And the Walls Came Tumbling Down: An Autobiography* New York: Harper & Row 1989, 339
6.
7. Hampton, Henry; Fayer, Steve. *Voices of Freedom: An Oral History of the Civil Rights Movement from the 1950s through the 1980s* New York: Bantam Books, 1990.
8. Lewis, John. *Walking with the Wind: A Memoir of the Movement* San Diego: Harcourt, Brace & Co.; 1998, 348
9. Lewis, John. *Walking with the Wind: A Memoir of the Movement* San Diego: Harcourt, Brace & Co.; 1998, 368
10. Boston.com
11. Bishop, Jim. *The Days of Martin Luther King* G.P. Putnam and Sons; 1971, 416

Chapter 14

1. Mann, Robert *The Walls of Jericho* New York, Harcourt Brace & Co., 1996.
2. Mann, Robert *The Walls of Jericho* New York, Harcourt Brace & Co., 1996.
3. Mann, Robert *The Walls of Jericho* New York, Harcourt Brace & Co., 1996.
4. Mann, Robert *The Walls of Jericho* New York, Harcourt Brace & Co., 1996, 456
5. Bishop, Jim. *The Days of Martin Luther King* G.P. Putnam and Sons; 1971, 416
6. Mann, Robert *The Walls of Jericho* New York, Harcourt Brace & Co., 1996, 458
7. "Eyes on the Prize" documentary interview
8. Kotz, Nick. *Judgment Days: Lyndon Baines Johnson, Martin Luther King Jr. and the Laws that Changed America* New York and Boston: Houghton Mifflin, 2005, 269
9. Kotz, Nick. *Judgment Days: Lyndon Baines Johnson, Martin Luther King Jr. and the Laws that Changed America* New York and Boston: Houghton Mifflin, 2005, 296
10. "Goldman, Eric. *The Tragedy of Lyndon Johnson* New York: Alfred A. Knopf, 1969, 319
11. Goldman, Eric. *The Tragedy of Lyndon Johnson* New York: Alfred A. Knopf, 1969, 322
12. "Eyes on the Prize" television documentary transcripts
13. Chesnut, J.L., Cass, Julia. *Black in Selma"* Giroux, 1990, 212.hand
14. "Eyes on the Prize" television documentary transcripts
15. White House telephone transcripts, March 18, 1965

16. Abernathy, Ralph David. *And the Walls Came Tumbling Down: An Autobiography* New York: Harper & Row 1989, 348
17. Mann, Robert *The Walls of Jericho* New York, Harcourt Brace & Co., 1996, 458

Chapter 15

1. Hampton, Henry; Fayer, Steve. "Voices of Freedom" *An Oral History of the Civil Rights Movement from the 1950s through the 1980s* New York: Bantam Books, 1990, 237.
2. Lesher, Stephan. "George Wallace: American Populist" Reading, PA.: Addison-Wesley; 1994, 336
3. "Lewis, John. "Walking with the Wind" *A Memoir of the Movement* San Diego: Harcourt, Brace & Co.; 1998, 356
4. Bishop, Jim. *The Days of Martin Luther King* G.P. Putnam and Sons; 1971, 394
5. Selma Times-Journal, Monday, March 22, 1965
6. Bishop, Jim. *The Days of Martin Luther King* G.P. Putnam and Sons; 1971, 369
7. Selma Daily Times Journal, Monday, March 22—Friday, March 26, 1965
8. Young, Andrew. "An Easy Burden" *The Civil Rights Movement and the Transformation of America* HarperCollins, 1996, 367.
9. The New York Times, March 26, 1965
10. Carson, Clayborne. "We Shall Overcome" *The Autobiography of Martin Luther King Jr.* New York: Warner Books, Inc. 1998, 284

11. Harlan, Louis. We Shall Overcome: Martin Luther King Jr. and the Black Freedom Struggle Edited by Peter Albert and Ronald Hoffman. New York: DaCapo Press. 1994, 6 4
12. Carson, Clayborne. "We Shall Overcome" *The Autobiography of Martin Luther King Jr.* New York: Warner Books, Inc. 1989, 283-4
13. White House telephone transcripts
14. Chalmers, David. *Backfire: How the Ku Klux Klan Helped the Civil Rights Movement* Bowman and Littlefield, 2003, 6 4
15. Abernathy, Ralph David. *And the Walls Came Tumbling Down: An Autobiography* New York: Harper & Row 1989, 360
16. Fairclough, Adam. *To Redeem the Soul of America: The Southern Christian Leadership Council and Martin Luther King* Athens: University of Georgia Press, 1987, 250

Chapter 16

1. Mann, Robert. *The Walls of Jericho* Harcourt & Co., 1996, 464
2. Mann, Robert. *The Walls of Jericho* Harcourt & Co., 1996, 465.
3. Saturday Evening Post, March, 1965
4. Landsberg, Brian. *Free at Last to Vote: The Alabama Origins of the 1965 Voting Rights Act* University of Kansas Press, 2007, 168
5. Landsberg, Brian. *Free at Last to Vote: The Alabama Origins of the 1965 Voting Rights Act* University of Kansas Press, 2007. 171-2

6. Mann, Robert. *The Walls of Jericho* Harcourt Brace & Co., 1996, 473.
7. White House telephone transcripts
8. Branch, Taylor. *At Canaan's Edge:America in the King Years, 1965-1968* New York: Simon & Schuster, 2006, 486
9. Garrow, David. *The Civil Rights Movement: Turning Points in World History* San Diego: Greenhaven Press, 2000, 184
10. Roberts, Gene; Klibanoff, Hank. *The Race Beat: The Press, the Civil Rights Struggle, and the Awakening of a Nation* New York: Vintage Books 2006, 394
11. Fairclough, Adam. *To Redeem the Soul of America: The Southern Christian Leadership Council and Martin Luther King* Athens: University of Georgia Press, 1987, 255
12. Lewis, John. *"Walking with the Wind" A Memoir of the Movemen.* San Diego: Harcourt, Brace & Co.; 1998

Chapter 17

1. The Anniston Star
2. National Public Radio interview transcripts, May 10, 2007
3. Circuit Court of Alabama, Perry County; CC-2007-17; November 8 and 9, 2007
4. Circuit Court of Alabama, Perry County; CC-2007-17; September 19, 2007

Chapter 18

1. Birmingham News, 2002
2. New York Times, June 2, 2010
3. Washington Post March 24, 2010
4. Fairclough, Adam. *To Redeem the Soul of America: The Southern Christian Leadership Council and Martin Luther King* Athens: University of Georgia Press, 1987, 254
5. "Eyes on the Prize" documentary transcripts

Afterword

1. Garrow, David. *Protest at Selma.* New Haven and London. Yale University Press, 1978, 21.

Made in the USA
Coppell, TX
08 February 2021

49950798R00152